THE REPUBLIC OF YEMEN

DEVELOPMENT CHALLENGES IN
THE 21ST CENTURY

Marta Colburn

STACEY INTERNATIONAL

First published 2002
Catholic Institute for International Relations (CIIR)
Unit 3 Canonbury Yard
190a New North Road
London N1 7BJ, UK

This edition published 2002
Stacey International
128 Kensington Church Street
London W8 4BH
Tel: (0)207 221 7166   Fax: (0) 207 792 9288
E-mail: enquiries@stacey-international.co.uk

ISBN: 1 900988 69 0

A CIP catalogue record for this book is available from the British Library

Edited by: Mara Stankovitch and Adam Bradbury
Designed by: Boldface, London
Printed by: Oriental Press
Cover picture: Marta Colborn

Contents

Tables

1. Geographic zones
2. Kingdoms of Ancient South Arabia
3. Major dynasties
4. The economy in the 1990s
5. Overview of major development assistance for 2000
6. Comparison of basic indicators: YAR, PDRY and ROY

Boxes

1. Sheik Sa'eed and the 'Gate of Lament'
2. Major events in Yemeni history
3. Cold War road race
4. An expensive vote
5. A snapshot of development challenges in the new millennium
6. A decade of consumer protest
7. The bitter pill of structural adjustment
8. The 1990s: The human cost
9. Water crisis in al-Sinah
10. The tragedy of inadequate health care
11. Shaykhly immunity
12. HIV/AIDS in Yemen
13. An Adeni voice: Nawal Anwar Khan
14. A biography of activism: Fatimah Huraybi Hassan
15. Comparing the lives of urban and rural women
16. International Cooperation for Development (ICD)

About the author

Marta Colburn has lived in Yemen periodically since 1984. From 1984 to 1989 she worked for a number of international development agencies, for the last two and a half years as Deputy Country Representative for Oxfam UK. From 1998 to 2000 she served as Resident Director of the American Institute for Yemeni Studies and, since March 2000, has worked as an independent consultant on a variety of projects in Yemen. Ms Colburn's education is in political science and Middle Eastern studies and for eight years she served as the Outreach Coordinator and Associate Director of the Middle East Studies Center at Portland State University. She has written on a range of topics related to Yemen including gender, democratisation and pre-collegiate curriculum. Among her experiences in Yemen are living with a Yemeni family for two years and marriage to a Yemeni. In 1999 she was kidnapped by tribesmen and held for 38 hours.

Author s note on text and Arabic transliteration

For foreign words, Yemen-specific terms and acronyms, see the glossary (page 78).

Transliterating Arabic in a consistent and readable manner is no easy task. For this document I have relied on commonly accepted English geographic terms and Arabic words that have made their way into the English lexicon. The standard transliteration for the 'ayn in English is ' (opening quotation mark) and for the glottal stop is ' (closing quotation mark). In this document I have not distinguished between the two. For readability I have refrained from using other diacritical marks.

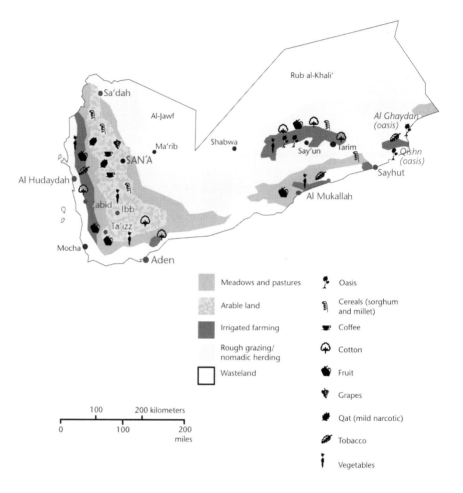

Rub al-Khali'

Sa'dah

Al-Jawf

Ma'rib

Shabwa

SAN'A

Al Hudaydah

Zabid   Ibb

Ta'izz

Mocha

Aden

Say'un   Tarim

Al Ghaydan (oasis)

Qishn (oasis)

Sayhut

Al Mukallah

	Meadows and pastures		Oasis
	Arable land		Cereals (sorghum and millet)
	Irrigated farming		Coffee
	Rough grazing/ nomadic herding		Cotton
	Wasteland		Fruit
			Grapes
			Qat (mild narcotic)
			Tobacco
			Vegetables

100   200 kilometers

0   100   200 miles

Shepherdess with her flock on the terraced slopes of the Hujariyyah.

MARTA COLBURN

Foreword

It gives me great pleasure to write the foreword for this publication by Marta Colburn for International Cooperation for Development (ICD). As this publication makes so clear, the development challenges for Yemen in the 21st century are significant.

However, it also clear that Yemen has a history rich in traditions which are in harmony with the natural environment and which build strong community.

Additionally, this book highlights the major development accomplishments since the revolution and independence struggles of the1960s.

Marta Colburn's nearly 20 years of studying Yemen and over eight years of living here are evident in her treatment of the subject. Also emerging from this impressive work is her great love for the people of Yemen and their rich and diverse culture.

It is fitting that ICD should produce this fine publication as they are one of the international development agencies with the longest presence in Yemen. While their projects have been small in scale, their contribution to Yemen's human development has been deeply appreciated.

I highly recommend this publication as furthering understanding of the Yemeni development experience.

Dr Abd al-Karim al-Iryani
Prime Minister of Yemen Arab Republic 1980-1983
and Republic of Yemen 1998-2001

BRUCE PALUCK

View from
KawKaban village.

DINNY HAWES/CIIR-ICD

San'a

INTRODUCTION

Some may associate Yemen with breathtaking architecture, or the Queen of Sheba, or the British-Yemeni boxing champion Prince Naseem. Unfortunately, much recent media coverage of this south west corner of the Arabian Peninsula has been negative. From tribal kidnapping to terrorism, it has emphasised the violent and unusual. This is a very narrow perspective on Yemen's rich cultural heritage and current realities. This report is intended to provide in-depth information and to outline the development challenges and opportunities facing the Yemeni people.

11 September 2001 will be engraved on our memories not only for the horror of what happened in the United States, and subsequently in Afghanistan, but also because of the profound impact of those events on international relations. In Yemen, where the government and people have been moving gradually towards democracy and an improving human rights record, these events are likely to have a far-reaching significance.

Against the background of the military campaign in Afghanistan, US officials included Yemen on a list of countries suspected of harbouring 'terrorists' and at the end of 2001 threatened direct military action. Justification for this action emphasised a spate of violent incidents in Yemen – bombing of the Gold Mohor hotel in Aden in 1993, in 1998 the first politically motivated kidnapping of 16 Western tourists (resulting in the death of four captives), and a fatal attack on the US ship *Cole* in October 2000. In addition, some al-Qa'eda members were believed to have fled from Afghanistan to Yemen.

In the wake of 11 September, and following a request from the US government, Yemen was swift to take internal action against 'terrorism'. President Ali Abdullah Saleh attended a meeting in Washington with President George W Bush and other senior US officials on 26 November 2001. The Yemeni government hastened to announce its cooperation with the United States to fight extremist elements in Yemen, and in return was offered a package of security and development assistance.

Specific actions taken include:
- The deportation of some 14,000 Arabs from Egypt, Algeria, Sudan, Libya, Saudi Arabia and Jordan;[a]
- Tightening up of visa requirements and other immigration procedures;
- The arrest and questioning of dozens of Yemenis suspected of having links to al-Qa'eda;
- Confiscation of thousands of audio tapes of Osama Bin Laden;
- In December 2001 becoming the first Muslim Arab government to take decisive military action against individuals identified by the US government as connected to al-Qa'eda, killing 24 and injuring 34 in Ma'rib and Shabwa;

a. *Yemen Times*, 24-30 September 2001

- Expanded cooperation with the United States in the USS Cole investigation'
- Sending a team of Yemeni investigators to Guatanamo Bay, Cuba;
- Bringing thousands of Islamic schools under the education ministry, enabling it to control the curriculum and the appointment and remuneration of teachers.

However, many analysts and Yemenis believe that the government's cooperation with the United States is the result of fear of military reprisals, economic hardship and marginalisation. If Yemen is not perceived as cooperating sufficiently the 'with us or against us' threat could translate badly for the country.

A sense of alienation and frustration among Yemenis has been shaped by many experiences over the years:

- Many Yemenis died fighting alongside Western-backed *mujahadeen* to expel the Soviet army from Afghanistan in the 1980s and 1990s. Yemenis also died with the Taliban during the US attacks on Afghanistan, and there is also strong sentiment over the deaths of Yemeni prisoners in Mazar al Sharif in circumstances that have not been fully explained.
- Although Yemeni Afghan Arabs returned to Yemen after the Soviet withdrawal from Afghanistan, their presence in Yemen bears little resemblance to that of al-Qa'eda found in Afghanistan prior to 11 September. Indeed, al-Qa-eda became known to most Yemenis only at the same time as the average American learned of it.
- A number of Yemenis have been killed in apparent hate-motivated incidents in the United States and Canada since 11 September.
- Yemenis are among the prisoners being held in controversial conditions in Camp X-Ray in Cuba.
- Yemenis have a deep interest in, and commitment to, a just resolution of the Palestinian-Israeli conflict and discuss the conflict daily at all levels. Many resent what they see as double standards in Western policies towards Islam and Arabs over other crises such as Bosnia, Chechnya and Somalia.
- Many people feel that Arab countries and their peoples have been deeply humiliated by bias in the handling of world crises.

The events of 11 September and after represent a setback for Yemen's emerging democracy movement. Champions of democratisation in Yemen now face a difficult task in explaining why Western democracies have formed alliances with some of the least democratic governments in the region.

Marta Colburn
Abdulla Al Syari, March 2002

Geography

Yemen is one of the oldest inhabited regions in the world. Archaeological evidence suggests that the first humans migrated to Yemen some 40,000 years ago. According to Arab and Yemeni tradition San'a', the capital city of the Republic of Yemen (ROY), was established by Shem, the son of Noah from the Old Testament flood. The ROY covers an area of approximately 555,000 sq km, twice the size of the United Kingdom. It stretches from the desert sands of the Rub' al-Khali (Empty Quarter) to mountain peaks 3,660 metres above sea level and drops back down to the coasts of the Red Sea and the Gulf of Aden. Yemen is separated from Africa by the strait of Bab al-Mandeb (meaning 'gate of lament'), whose narrowest point is 32 km across. The country is located between the latitudes of 12° 40' North and 19° North and between longitudes 42° 30' East and 53° East. It can be divided into six distinct geographic zones with associated climates, flora and fauna (see Table 1 below). Additionally, Yemen embraces 112 islands (some of them inhabited) in the Red and Arabian Seas. Historical events as well as the physical geography of these zones have shaped human lifestyles and agrarian traditions.

Table 1. Geographic zones

Zone	Elevation range	Approximate annual rainfall	Additional comments
1. Coastal	0-200 m	0-100 mm	Wadi agriculture, larger land holdings with a high proportion of sharecropping
2. Western escarpment	200-1,500 m	300-1,000 mm	Terraced rain-fed farming ideal for coffee and qat, some sharecropping
3. Northern highlands	1,500-3,600 m	100-500 mm	Subsistence farming, irrigation on the plateaus, predominantly tribal
4. Southern highlands	1,500-2,500 m	300-1,500 mm	Irrigated and rain fed, densely populated, some sharecropping
5. Eastern slopes	1,500-1,000 m	50-200 mm	Predominantly wadi agriculture, otherwise scarcely populated pastoral/ nomadic lifestyle
6. Desert	500-1,000 m	0-50 mm	Sparse population sustaining largely pastoral/ nomadic lifestyle

1 HISTORICAL BACKGROUND

The ROY was created on 22 May 1990 with the unification of the Yemen Arab Republic (YAR – also referred to as North Yemen) and the People's Democratic Republic of Yemen (PDRY – also referred to as South Yemen). Pre-unification history can be divided into five periods: ancient Yemen, the early Islamic period (from the rise of Islam until the 16th century), the era of European struggles for dominance in the region, modern history (the early 20th century) and the republican era, from the 1960s to 1990.

Ancient Yemen

Archaeological evidence of advanced irrigation and agrarian systems in Yemen dates back as far as the third millennium BC. By the 6th century BC, Yemen sustained a highly developed culture capable of producing the 680-metre long, 16-metre high Ma'rib dam that irrigated an estimated 9,600 hectares.[1] Twenty thousand people helped repair its partially destroyed structure in 450 AD.[2] Advanced political, social, cultural and economic systems enabled successive Yemeni civilisations to control trade routes across the Arabian Peninsula between the Far East and the Mediterranean. In addition to transporting luxury products from Asia and Africa, from the 1st millennium BC enormous camel caravans also carried frankincense and myrrh grown in ancient Yemen (present day Oman – zone 6 on the map). Since the earliest recorded times in Sumeria, Babylonia and Egypt the aromatic resins of the frankincense and myrrh trees have been burnt as incense for practical, ritual and symbolic purposes. Observing the wealth of goods coming out of ancient South Arabia the Romans referred to the area as 'Arabia Felix' (happy, or blessed Arabia).

The most powerful of Yemen's ancient civilizations was that of Saba', or Sheba, which ruled much of Yemen from the 10th century BC to 6th century AD. It was the Sabaeans who built the Ma'rib dam and, according to Arab and Islamic

Table 2. Kingdoms of ancient South Arabia

Kingdom	Approximate dates	Area of influence
Sabaean	10th century BC to 6th century AD	Ma'rib & al-Jawf
Awasan	7th to 5th centuries BC	Wadi Markhah
Ma'in	7th century BC to 1st century AD	al-Jawf
Qataban	5th century BC to 1st century AD	Bayhan
Hadhramaut	5th century BC to 3rd century AD	Wadi Hadhramaut and Shabwa
Himyar	2nd century BC to 6th century AD	North and south highlands

1. The population of ancient Ma'rib is estimated at between 100,000 and 250,000 (Dr Christopher Edens).
2. Brunner (1985), pp52 and 54.

traditions, Bilquis the Queen of Sheba was their most famous ruler. Her reputation was built not only on her wealth and beauty, but also on her wisdom and relationship with King Solomon. The Queen of Sheba has the distinction of being the only queen mentioned in the sacred texts of Judaism, Christianity and Islam.[3] While clear evidence has yet to emerge that she really existed, and about whether she ruled from ancient Ethiopia or the Arabian Peninsula, she plays an important role in Yemeni conceptions of their ancient history.

In the 1st century AD the Romans learned that many luxuries reaching them from South Arabia actually came from Asia. More importantly, they discovered the secret of sailing the monsoon winds. Sea routes quickly replaced the land routes and the influence of ancient South Arabian civilisations waned with subsequent events: the rise of Christianity (and its early prohibition of incense); foreign invasions and brief occupations by the Ethiopian Axumite Empire (4th and 6th centuries AD) and the Persian Sassanid Empire (575-628 AD); the final collapse of the Ma'rib dam in the 6th century AD; and a lack of leadership coupled with internal political fragmentation.

Early Islam in Yemen

South Arabian influence in trade waned, but Yemen's importance revived with the rise of Islam. Many Yemeni leaders and their tribes converted to Islam in the 7th century AD, leading the Prophet Mohammed to proclaim to his entourage, 'People have come to you from Yemen. They are the most amiable and gentle hearted of men. Faith is of Yemen, and wisdom is Yemeni.' Mosques built in San'a' and al-Janad were among the first in Islam and Yemeni troops were crucial in the expansion of the Islamic empire. Despite this central role in early Islam, as the empire expanded its centre moved from the Arabian Peninsula to other locations. However, through invasions and alliances Yemen remained connected to political and economic developments in the broader Islamic empire. It also produced religious scholars, artists, mathematicians and scientists. A 13th century Yemeni Rasulid Sultan, al-Ashraf 'Umar, is probably the only king in history to construct and write a treatise on a major scientific instrument – the astrolabe (used to observe celestial bodies and to calculate Muslim prayer times using trigonometry).[4]

In 896 AD local tribes invited al-Hadi ila al-Haqq Yahya ibn Husayn to Yemen as an arbitrator. This dynamic individual inaugurated the Zaydi[5] Shi'ah Imamate (theocratic rule) that controlled much of the northern highlands and other parts of Yemen for nearly a millennium. It was during this period that Yemen's religious diversity evolved through events including the arrival of descendants of the Prophet Mohammed (through his daughter Fatimah and her husband 'Ali). Collectively this group is known by several names depending on their lineage: 'Alawis (descendents of 'Ali), *sadah* (plural of *sayyid*) or *ashraf* (plural of *sharif*). This religious elite of Adnani (northern Arab) tribal ancestry arrived in Yemen at the end of the 9th century. In 1967 it was estimated that there were 200,000–300,000 *sadah* in Yemen with particularly high numbers in the Wadi Hadhramaut.

3. I Kings 10: 1-13; II Chronicles 9: 1-12; and the Holy Qur'an, *Surat al-Naml*, No. 27, and *Surat Saba'*, No. 34.

4. Today al-Ashraf's astrolabe is in the Metropolitan Museum of Art in New York.

5. Zaydism is a Shi'ah school of Islamic jurisprudence that was established by Zayd ibn 'Ali, a grandson of Husayn, the fifth Imam in Islam.

Table 3. Major dynasties

Dynasty	Dates (AD)	Area of Influence
Zayadid	818-1021	Northern Tihamah
Ya'furid	839-1003	San'a'
Zaydi	896-1962	Various
Najahid	1022-1159	Northern Tihamah
Sulayhid	1038-1138	All of Yemen
Ayyubid	1174-1229	All of Yemen
Rasulid	1229-1454	All of Yemen
Tahirid	1454-1526	Tihamah and southern highlands
Kathiri	1489-1967	Wadi Hadhramaut
	1489-1858	coast and west Wadi
Abdali	1728-1839	Aden
	1728-1967	Lahj
Qu'ayti	1858-1967	Coast and west Wadi Hadhramaut
Fadhli	1887-1967	Abyan and Shabwa

Yemen at the crossroads

During the 16th century Yemen's location at the crossroads of Asia, Africa and Europe took on new meaning as the great powers of the day sought to expand their spheres of influence. Over the next four centuries, the Portuguese, Dutch, British, Italian, French and Americans as well as the Ottoman Turks, Omanis and others, competed for control in the region. In 1507 the Portuguese annexed the island of Soqotra in the Arabian Sea and in 1513 they attacked Aden. A flurry of commercial and military activity prompted the Mamluk empire in Egypt to protect its interests by invading the Tihamah and a portion of Yemen's highlands in 1517. In 1538 the Ottoman empire assumed the mantle of Islamic imperial leadership from the Mamluks and gained direct control of Yemen. In 1636 the Zaydi Imamate succeeded in evicting the Ottomans and extended its influence over much of the country for the next two centuries. However, the British annexation of Aden in 1839 prompted the Ottomans to reassert their authority in Yemen by invading the Tihamah in 1849. The opening of the Suez Canal in 1869 ensured the importance of Aden's port for the British and enabled the Ottomans to bring more troops to expand their occupation in the north. Despite continued local resistance, the Ottoman occupation continued until the end of the First World War. British influence slowly spread into the hinterland of southern Yemen through treaties with local rulers.

A commercial sensation of this period was coffee. This drink was introduced to the world via the Red Sea port of al-Mocha and brought Yemen back into international commerce for the first time since the demise of the incense trade. The coffee plant is native to the Horn of Africa as well as to Yemen, but it was Yemeni Sufi mystics in the late 13th or early 14th century who first brewed and consumed coffee to enhance their spiritual endeavours. By the 15th century coffee was widely consumed in Yemen and the 16th century Ottoman occupation of Yemen brought the drink to Europe. By the mid-17th century coffee was being consumed in Vienna, Amsterdam, London and New York. However, by the end of the 17th century the Europeans had broken Yemen's monopoly by smuggling out coffee trees and cultivating them in their own colonies in East Asia, East Africa and Latin America.

In 1890, a new Zaydi Imam, Mohammed ibn Yahya Hamid al-Din, rose to power. His diplomatic skills and military prowess posed a serious threat to both Ottoman and British interests.

Modern history

In 1904 Imam Mohammed died and was succeeded by his son Yahya who continued, with others in Yemen, to resist the Turkish and British empires. With the Ottoman defeat in the First World War and withdrawal from Yemen in 1918, Yemen was the first Arab country to gain independence. In 1933-34 Yemen and the newly established Kingdom of Saudi Arabia went to war and the Saudis occupied the Yemeni provinces of Najran, 'Asir and Jizan. Under the 1934 Ta'if Treaty, Yemen temporarily suspended its historic claim to this territory. This military defeat served as a catalyst for the Imam to modernise his government, in particular the military. He sent about a dozen young men to Iraq for military training in 1936. On their return, they joined other Yemenis in agitating for reform and modernisation of the country's military, social, political, economic and administrative systems. The Free Yemeni Movement, born in the mid-1940s, led an unsuccessful coup attempt in 1948 that left Imam Yahya dead and his eldest son Ahmed in power. Imam Ahmed continued his father's policy of

---

1. SHEIK-SA'EED AND THE 'GATE OF LAMENT'

Sheikh Sa'eed on the southern coast of the Bab al-Mandeb ('gate of lament') was an important port in ancient Yemen that had been forgotten by history until the Red Sea regained some of its importance in the 17th century. As the great powers of the day began to compete in the area the local tribe of Akemi-ed-Durein turned the situation to their advantage. A French company purchased the port of Sheikh Sa'eed and some 400,000 acres of adjacent land from the tribe. A letter to editors in the National Geographic Magazine in 1897 highlights the various interests operating in the region and claiming 'ownership' of the port. The author Ernest De Sasseville, a Frenchman, noted that the port of Sheikh Sa'eed was described as a French, British and Turkish territory, depending on the map consulted. He writes that this confusion 'furnishes an example of inaccurate map-making by men who are apparently more zealous and patriotic than learned and accurate. Whatever may be said of the claims of France to the territory in question, it does not appear that England has ever had the shadow of a claim to it, and Mr Phillip (the mapmaker who listed it as British territory) ought to know that the use of a brush and some colour to make a territory appear to be either English, French, or Turkish, according to one's patriotic ambitions, does not make it so.'

Based on *National Geographic Magazine* (1897) 'Sheik Said', pp155-6. The port of Sheikh Sa'eed is on the north west side of the Bab al-Mandeb peninsula, and is today called Ra's Sheikh Sa'eed. Owing to changes in the Red Sea coastline, the port is now silted up and suitable only for fishing vessels. (Thanks to David Stanton for clarification.)

isolation and gradual modernisation, and popular discontent continued, resulting in a number of failed assassination and coup attempts. Imam Ahmed's death (of natural causes) in 1962 gave rise to a leadership crisis, and various groups led by the Iraqi-trained officers declared the YAR on 26 September 1962.

Unrest in the hinterland and the threat of Turkish and Zaydi influence prompted the British to expand their interests in the south. British affairs in south Arabia were directed from India until 1937, when the Aden Colony was officially proclaimed and the Eastern and Western Protectorates were established. The British expanded their military and administrative control, and provided some education and health services. Southern Yemenis, particularly in Aden, enjoyed some advantages over their northern Zaydi-ruled neighbours, and the language of self-governance, independence and modernisation spreading around the globe was also heard in South Yemen. From the start, British rule encountered opposition in rural communities and among the tribes and, after the Second World War, increasingly in Aden. In the 1950s and 1960s many organisations actively resisted British rule. In 1963 the National Liberation Front (NLF) was founded and when the British withdrew from Aden on 30 November 1967, its leaders declared the birth of the PDRY.

The republican era

In the north, the YAR was far from stable. Independence was followed by a civil war that embroiled regional and international powers until 1970. In the first 15 years of the republic's existence, two out of five presidents were assassinated.[6] The assumption of power by President 'Ali 'Abdullah Saleh in 1978 brought a degree of stability and steady improvements in human and economic development through the 1980s. However, the administrative and political weakness of the central government, combined with tribal independence, meant that state control was minimal outside urban centres and the San'a'-Hodeidah-Ta'izz triangle.

In the south, the NLF found itself in control of a nearly bankrupt country. There was no more British financial assistance, and Aden lost 75 per cent of its port revenues when the 1967 Arab-Israeli War closed the Suez Canal. The NLF rapidly transformed itself from a liberation organisation into a socialist government, becoming the Yemeni Socialist Party (YSP) in 1978. Until the early 1980s, domestic politics in the PDRY were typified by infighting among the ruling elite, often ending in violence; two out of five presidents met violent ends[7] and the civil war of 1986 killed thousands. However, during its 23 years of independence state legal and administrative systems became relatively developed throughout the PDRY, facilitating the delivery of government services such as education and health care.

While there were economic differences between the YAR and PDRY, by the 1980s significant similarities had developed. These include the importance of agriculture (28 per cent and 16 per cent of gross domestic product respectively), relatively weak industrial sectors (17 per cent and 23 per cent of GDP) and balance of payments problems. Both states spent heavily on defence and security (54 per cent and 43 per cent)[8] and relied on external aid to subsidise development efforts. In 1987 official development assistance (ODA) represented 8.1 per cent of the YAR's gross national product (GNP) and 8.2 per cent of the GNP of the PDRY.[9]

6. Abdullah al-Sallal 1962-67; Abd al-Rahman al-Iryani 1967-74; Ibrahim al-Hamdi 1974-77 (assassinated); the brief rule of Ahmed al-Ghashmi 1977-78 (assassinated); Ali Abdullah Saleh 1978-90.
7. Qahtan ash-Shaabi 1967-1969; Salem Rubaya Ali 1969-1978 (executed); Ali Nasr Mohammed 1978 and again from 1980 to 1986; Abdul Fattah Ismail 1978-1980 (killed during 1986 civil war); and Haidar Abu Bakr al-Attas 1986-1990.
8. Data from 1987 (Carapico 1998, p40).
9. Bilateral assistance from Arab countries to the PDRY peaked in 1982 with US$126 million in grants and US$600 million in loans. Assistance to the YAR peaked in 1980 at well over US$1 billion from global, regional, bilateral and multilateral donors; by 1985 it had dropped to less than half a billion, and in 1988 to less than US$100 million. (*Ibid*).

The economies were also dominated by migrant labour remittances. It is estimated that at the height of the remittance boom in the late 1970s and early 1980s more than one-third of the male labour force worked outside the country.[10] In 1982 these workers sent home more than $1 billion annually to the YAR; in the PDRY it was estimated that remittances accounted for more than half of GNP.[11] Although oil was discovered in modest quantities in the YAR in 1984 and in the PDRY in 1986, a lack of infrastructure, lawlessness in oil-producing areas, corruption and bureaucratic inefficiency have limited its impact on living standards.

Conclusion

One theme that has remained important throughout Yemeni history is tribalism. Historically, south Arabian tribes were rarely nomads, but rather warriors who were settled cultivators working their own land. Tribes in Yemen are defined by genealogy, geography and occupation, with a history of cooperation within tribes and between neighbouring tribes. Tribalism (or *qabyala*) is defined as a complex system of laws, behaviours and values prescribed and agreed by members, complete with political and military structures. Moreover, tribalism contains a collective identity and a perception of non-tribal elements of society. Tribal values include those of a warrior – courage, bravery and endurance – as well as generosity, pride, faithfulness to one's word, autonomy, industriousness, and knowledge, piety and respect for tribal customs.[12]

The tribes of Yemen trace their ancestry back to Qahtan, reputedly a descendant of Noah. In ancient times the tribe constituted the structure of the state. However, with the collapse of the ancient South Arabian kingdoms tribes fragmented. During the past few centuries in both north and south, state-tribal relations were characterised by temporary alliances, dictated by necessity or prudence and fraught with mutual distrust. This inherent tension was usually surmounted through a variety of tactics designed by the central government (the British in the south and the Imam in the north) to ensure tribal cooperation. In the 20th century, the Imamate kept tribes in the northern parts of the country under nominal control through a system of rewards,[13] punishments[14] and deterrence, and by fomenting dissent between tribes. Despite the instability of this period, northern tribes remained independent entities governed by their own leadership, with recognised boundaries and codes of behaviour.

10. Immigration from Yemen, largely for economic reasons, is an ancient practice dating back to the collapse of the Ma'rib dam. The Wadi Hadhramaut is particularly famous for this tradition. Sir Richard Burton once stated that 'It is generally said that the sun does not rise upon a land that does not contain a man from Hadhramaut.' Yemeni ports served as a conduit for migration abroad and the British colonial presence in Aden provided excellent opportunities for those who desired to seek their fortunes abroad. Destinations for Yemeni migrant workers varied over time and according to their place of origin, level of skills, prior connections and trends in immigration opportunities. Significant transient and permanent communities of Yemenis exist today in the United States, Britain, Africa (primarily Ethiopia, Kenya, Somalia and the Sudan), India, Malaysia, Indonesia, Singapore, the Gulf States and Saudi Arabia. In Ethiopia in the post-Second World War period it is estimated that there were 300,000-400,000 Yemenis, many of whom returned to Yemen at the time of the 1973-74 change of government.

11. *Ibid*, p34.

12. Adra (1985) p277.

13. Rewards included payments of arms, money or agricultural lands, as well as allowing the tribes to loot urban areas (for example, in 1948 tribes were allowed to sack the city of San'a' as punishment for inhabitants' collaboration in the assassination of Imam Yahya).

14. One such punishment was the Imamate practice of taking sons, or family members, of tribal leaders hostage in the capital. If the tribe of a 'guest' opposed the Imam's authority the hostage was killed. (Manea 1998, p3.)

The two most significant tribal confederations in Yemen today are the Hashid and Bakil. Tracing their history back to ancient Yemen, these two groupings reside in the northern highlands surrounding San'a', reaching north and east to the Saudi Arabian border. The Hashid Confederation comprises seven major tribes which are very cohesive and organised and since 1959 has been led by *shaykh* 'Abdullah bin Husayn al-Ahmar (referred to as their paramount *shaykh* – *shaykh al-mashayikh*). The Bakil Confederation numbers 15 loosely confederated tribes nominally led by *shaykh* Naji bin 'Abd al-'Aziz al-Shayif.[15] A third historic tribal confederation is Madhhij, currently numbering four tribes, but in the process of regrouping, potentially to include some south Yemeni tribes with ancient connections. The tribes in southern Yemen are either attached to separate groupings from Shabwah to Oman, or stand in splendid isolation like the Yafi' tribe, sometimes referred to as 'the Hashid of the South'.[16]

Tribal traditions which date back millennia are changing fundamentally, for various reasons. Since unification the government has reinvigorated tribal structures in areas that had gradually moved away from their tribal roots, often with disturbing results.[17] Another change is that tribal values that traditionally controlled the incidence of violence are disintegrating. The estimated 50 million weapons in Yemen make it one of the most heavily armed populations in the world. Kidnapping, tribally related violence and incidents involving guns[18] regularly violate the sacredness of Yemen's *hijar*.[19] Yet another impetus for change in Yemeni tribalism is urbanisation. Yemen's population explosion combined with limited land[20] and water[21] has forced many *qaba'il* to move to urban areas, which offer greater opportunities for education, health care, employment and leisure. While this has been a positive change for many it has also eroded tribal values, particularly for younger generations who are raised with little meaningful connection to their tribal past. The urban environment has also radically changed tribal women's lives, with access to bottled gas, piped water, indoor plumbing and relief from their agricultural burden. However, the transition from female farmers to urban housewives also brings isolation and boredom, reduced mobility and increased pressure to maintain family honour in a non-tribal milieu.

In conclusion, while tribal legal traditions, political structures, military capabilities and social norms greatly influence life in Yemen, this obvious fact obscures the complexity of society. Today, tribal behavior and values are largely limited to the northern part of the country where they have maintained their

---

15. Dresch (1995), p37 and pp47-8.
16. For an in-depth study of tribes in Yemen see Dresch (1989).
17. See Carapico (1998), pp163-4 for description of tribal conferences in 1990 that reaffirmed and awoke tribal affiliations within a party context.
18. In June of 1999 the government renewed its campaign to disarm citizens within city limits in an attempt to reduce tribally motivated violence. In the first month of the ban authorities claim that over 13,000 weapons were confiscated. Salah Haddash, a lawyer, reported that in 1996 there were 1,257 incidents related to blood revenge. According to Ministry of Interior statistics, during the first six months of 1999, 117 people were killed and 250 wounded in armed clashes and robberies (Lowry and Henin, 2000, pp50-1).

19. *Hijar* (plural of *hijrah*) meaning protected or sacred enclaves/settlements. See page 23 below for a discussion of Yemen's urban *hijar*
20. Only 2.9 per cent (1.6 million hectares) of Yemen is prime cultivatable land with another 3.7 per cent (2 million hectares) of marginal land (Republic of Yemen, 2000, IPRSP, p3).
21. Per capita water supply is about 2 per cent of the world average and 85 per cent below levels needed for domestic use. While most farmland is rain fed, groundwater irrigation (particularly for production of *qat*, a shrub whose leaves are chewed to produce a mildly stimulating euphoric sensation), exacerbated by government subsidies on diesel fuel, has jeopardised this resource which is also the primary source for domestic use (*Ibid*).

political influence. Outside the confederations many rural areas (particularly in the southern uplands and on the coast) that historically wielded tribal influence can no longer use their tribal structures in the political arena. When compared to the influence and cohesion of the northern confederations their tribal affiliations at the national level are largely symbolic.

2. MAJOR EVENTS IN YEMENI HISTORY

BC

c. 40,000	First evidence of human migration to Yemen
c. 5000	First evidence of settlements in the Yemeni highlands
6th century	Construction of the Ma'rib dam
1st century	San'a' becomes a major centre of inland trade

AD

1st century	Romans learn to sail the monsoon winds
6th century	Destruction of the Ma'rib dam
7th century	Rise of Islam; Yemeni tribes convert to Islam
896	Zaydi presence established in the highlands
1547-1636	First Ottoman occupation of Yemen
Early C16th	Coffee exported from the port of Mocha in Yemen arrives in Europe via the Ottomans
End C17th	European powers break Yemen's coffee monopoly
1839	British occupation of Aden
1869	Suez Canal opened
1871-1918	Second Ottoman occupation of Yemen
1933-34	War between Yemen and Saudi Arabia: Yemen cedes northern provinces in the Ta'if Treaty
1936	Imam Yahya sends young men to Iraq for military training

1937	The Aden Protectorate is established, divided into the Western and Eastern Protectorates
1948	Imam Yahya assassinated by Free Yemeni Movement
1962	Imam Ahmed dies; his son Badr rules for six days before Yemeni independence is declared
1962-1970	Civil war in North Yemen between Royalist and Republican forces
1967	British forces leave Aden and the NLF declares the People's Republic of South Yemen (PRSY), to become the PDRY in 1970
1971,72, 78,79,88	Tensions between the YAR and PDRY erupt in armed conflict
1978	'Ali 'Abdullah Saleh becomes President of the YAR
1980s	Oil is discovered in the YAR (1984) and PDRY (1986)
1990	Unification: the YAR and PDRY become the ROY
1990-91	Iraq invades Kuwait and the Gulf War ensues – expulsion of Yemeni workers from Saudi Arabia and the Gulf states and suspension of assistance from the United States, Saudi Arabia and Kuwait
1993/97	Nationwide parliamentary elections, deemed largely 'free and fair'
1994	Civil war
1995	ROY government undertakes economic reform with international donor support

c. = Circa
Compiled from *Burrowes Historical Dictionary of Yemen* (1995b) and Serjeant and Lewcock, eds, (1983) *San'a': An Arabian Islamic City*.

PART 2
DEVELOPMENT

View of Shibam, Wadi Hadhramaut, from Suhail.

II INDIGENOUS TRADITIONS AND DEVELOPMENT

In the process of economic and human development, traditions that have sustained communities for thousands of years can often be eclipsed. Ignorance of local traditions and belief in the superiority of modernity often destroy sustainable indigenous practices. For example, the first westerners to arrive in Yemen described a local practice of effective inoculation with blood from individuals who had survived smallpox, long before this technique was 'discovered' in the West. Highlighted below are a few indigenous traditions that continue into the modern era.

Consultation and consensus

Yemen has strong traditions promoting consultation and consensus in decision making. Historically rooted in Islam and tribalism, they retain their meaning in the lives of many Yemenis. Popular sovereignty in Islam is clearly supported by the principles of mutual consultation (*shurah*), consensus (*ijma*) and independent interpretive judgment (*ijtihad*). These principles date from the earliest days of Islam and are embodied in the actions and model of the Prophet Mohammed. Although these terms have other uses in Muslim discourse, contemporary Islamic scholars and leaders have used them as foundations in their endeavours to democratise their societies. The mutual agreement of equals is generally the basis for the democratic process of electing tribal leaders. Moreover, consultation and consensus-building are a recognised component of the decision-making process within and among tribes. These practices are time-consuming, but they generally result in decisions that reflect community ownership. Since his rise to power in the YAR in 1978, President 'Ali 'Abdullah Saleh's leadership style has been typified by the consultation and consensus of tribal leadership, thus contributing to stability and facilitating Yemen's transition to democracy.

Traditional consensus-building practices are also evident when tribes consider their interests vis-à-vis outside actors such as the state. Gatherings of tribal leaders allow each tribe to express its concerns in the process of arriving at a collective position. Conferences of tribes have been a facet of contemporary Yemeni politics since the early 1960s.[22] In the 1990s many tribal gatherings addressed issues of common national concern. The National Cohesion Conference (1991), the Saba' Conference (1992) and the United Bakil Conference (1994) developed resolutions on a range of topics but, according to the anthropologist Paul Dresch, included common points. For example:

- 'First, none makes a claim to tribal precedence. Indeed all of them insist that tribalism is a matter of equality and that promoting people on the grounds of shared tribal membership is wrong…
- 'Second, all of them insist on administrative reform…

22. Dresch (1995), pp44-45.

- 'Third, the disputes and bloodshed that others often blame on the tribes are blamed by all tribal meetings on the state...
- 'Fourth, reform of the state apparatus is a constant demand, as it has been in many quarters. (Far from rejecting the state, let alone a particular government, the tribes have been demanding that they be treated decently as citizens; there is no doubt whatsoever of their national loyalty.)
- 'Finally, although the party preferences of those involved differ hugely, all the meetings insist upon strict neutrality with regard to party claims. (Tribalism appears as a means of constraining the excesses of factionalism, yet still allows tribes people to take part freely in the wider forms of national politics.)'[23]

Although it is difficult to judge the impact of these gatherings on national politics, it is clear that the ability of the tribes to act collectively has been important and remains so. When united on an issue, these well-armed groups pose a credible threat to central government. This has had both positive (moderating excessive state force) and negative (the weakness of the rule of law – see Chapter V, section 2) consequences.

Mediation, negotiation and conflict resolution

Conflict is inevitable in human relations. Yemeni history is rich in Islamic and tribal practices of mediation, negotiation and conflict resolution. Tribe members understand that conflict can disrupt the community, particularly when the parties are heavily armed.[24] Tribal conflicts are not always peacefully resolved, but Yemeni tribal society has mechanisms for containing and minimising the impact of violence. When a conflict develops among members of a tribe, or between different tribes, over boundaries, land, inheritance or honour, there are carefully prescribed ways of resolving it.

Conflict resolution techniques vary between tribes and places, and according to the circumstances of each case. However, the methods are generally time-honoured and all include parties to the conflict agreeing on a respected arbiter. The selection of this individual is the first step in resolving the conflict. Arbitrators use their skill with words, knowledge of legal traditions (both 'urf, customary law, and shari'ah, Islamic or canonical law), conflict resolution techniques, wisdom and reputation for persuasion and negotiation. Tribal legal codes ('urf) provide guidelines for guarantees that parties will suspend hostilities, compensation for damage, mediation protocols and standards of right and wrong. General consensus on these elements is required, as the cooperation of other tribe members is essential to resolve the conflict. Paul Dresch provides an example of the role of surety as a temporary means of restoring the 'balance' between parties to a conflict.

A shaykh who is called on to arbitrate takes surety from the ghurama' or disputing parties. In a minor case they simply lay their daggers before him to demand an opinion, but in more complex matters he will retain these daggers, or much more usually a rifle from each, until he can resolve their claims; and so long as these tokens are held, any offence by one of the disputing parties against the other or against the 'arbitrator' is 'ayb (disgrace or insult).[25]

23. Ibid, p53.
24. It is estimated that Yemen is home to some 50 million weapons, making its population one of the most heavily armed in the world.
25. Dresch (1993), p92.

The laying down of a valued item is extremely common; it may be a dagger, rifle, or in the case of urban educated (unarmed) men disputing literature or geography, a watch. This symbolic action imposes obligations on the arbitrator to find an equitable solution, and on the parties to the dispute to respect the arbitrator's judgement.[26]

The sacred enclave

The historical settled agriculture of Yemeni tribes required them to build working relations with other tribes, and protected parties within their territory are essential to their prosperity. One important aspect of this 'peaceful coexistence' is the pre-Islamic tradition of the sacred enclave, variously called *hijrah*, *haram* and *hawtah*. Many towns and cities in Yemen have *hijrah* status – San'a', Sa'dah, 'Amran, Khamir, Kawkaban, Shibam, Tarim and Manakha. These cities and market towns functioned as neutral territory and home to many of the religious elites, scholars, judges and service providers. Also, tribally protected groups, such as Jews, usually settled in these enclaves. The relationship of the tribe members to the traders and the religious elite is one of mutual dependence. According to the scholar R B Serjeant, 'the little city states of Arabia are the natural outcome of the economic and political needs of the tribal peoples whose interest it is to keep them protected from violence and robbery. Protection may be given with the added sanction of religion – by making a town or village a sacred enclave. Or it may be purely secular, as when a tribal lord guarantees the security of the market…City and countryside are interdependent – the tribes cannot long do without the city – the city cannot function without the goodwill of the tribes around it.'[27]

The importance of the *hijrah* tradition is shown by the example of a dispute between two tribes in a *wadi* in the far east of Yemen. Both tribes had traditionally grazed their animals there but 'water was found and each claimed the area was theirs to farm. When the dispute reached violent deadlock, one of the suggestions made was that the place be 'made *hijrah*', meaning no one from either side could encroach on it without incurring a penalty. A still-point (ceasefire) was to be formed and upheld until agreement could be reached on what to do with the disputed area and its resources.'[28] The 'sacredness' and intrinsic protection of the *hijrah* can also be granted by mutual agreement to individuals and families, as is the case with some *mashayikh* and their families.

Community self-help and solidarity

Cooperation among tribespeople is one of the defining values of the tribe. This is reinforced by Islamic patterns of charitable giving and principles that reinforce community solidarity and self-help. Examples include the Islamic traditions of *zakat*[29] and *sadaqa*,[30] mutual support among farmers, charitable giving to victims of natural disasters or tragic events and sharing with friends and family to pay for weddings and other major expenses.[31] The principle of community cooperation found expression in Local Development Associations (LDAs) first established in the Ta'izz area of North Yemen in the 1940s. During the 1970s and 1980s in the YAR, popularly elected LDAs were established throughout the country with

26. Ibid, pp113-114.
27. Serjeant (1977), pp127-128.
28. Dresch (1993), p148.
29. *Zakat*, or alms-giving, is one of the five obligations of Muslims. In Yemen one's *zakat* payment is 5 per cent of net resources calculated annually and paid to poor individuals and families.
30. *Sadaqa* consists of voluntary contributions throughout the year of food, money, clothes, and so on, to those less fortunate.
31. For a summary of self-help traditions see ROY *et al*, *Children and Women in Yemen: A Situation Analysis 1998*, Vol I, p13.

varying degrees of government involvement and sponsorship (considerably more during the al-Hamdi era). The LDAs collected funds and in-kind support from residents, non-resident migrant labourers, external donors and the government. LDAs formalised mutual self-help traditions and enabled local communities to build and improve roads, schools, water projects, health facilities and other development schemes.[32]

The LDAs continued to operate until 1984, when the central government became unable to pay for projects. In 1985 they were merged with the central government's locally-based administrative structure, transforming them into Local Councils for Cooperative Development (LCCDs). These were given larger budgets but less flexibility in decision making and they were subject to greater central control.[33] During the late 1980s the LCCDs increasingly came to be directed from the centre and lost their earlier community-based character. After unification the LCCDs and the PDRY's local popular councils became branches of the Ministry of Local Administration, although community activists continued to lobby for revitalisation of the system. Widespread popular support for community-based govenance and decentralisation led to the passing of the Local Administration Law No. 4 (2000). This Law grants significant local power in decision making and resource allocation to local councils composed of appointed and elected members. The first nationwide elections to the local councils were held in February 2001. Implementing the decentralisation process is a complex task, but it could increase popular participation in governance.

Other traditions of community self-help and solidarity include *al-Ana*, or *al-Shamla*, voluntary work by community members to build wells, bridges, dams and other public works. This tradition is invoked after natural disasters to help feed and clothe the victims, or when the sick or elderly need help to harvest their crops. Although the work is supposed to be voluntary, penalties are often levied on those who are able but unwilling to help.[34] Another example found in both rural and urban communities is that of *al-Ghrum*, the provision of assistance to the victims (individuals or families) of an accident. 'There are two main types of *ghrum*: 1) blood *ghrum* is raised from the extended families and relatives to pay compensation for unintentional problems such as a road accident; and 2) state and property *ghrum* is collected by members of a particular class of workers such as traders and farmers, to help those in their own group during misfortune. Contributions are compulsory but payment is made according to means.'[35]

Water conservation

As an agricultural society in an environment where water is relatively scarce, Yemen has witnessed millennia of creative conservation of water for human use. In ancient times the Ma'rib dam gave Yemen a reputation for innovative use of limited water resources. The mountain slopes of Yemen are regularly drenched by the Indian Ocean monsoons. Yemenis have designed many ways to store water until it is needed, or engineered systems to bring water to where it can be used. It is estimated that Yemenis harness one-quarter of their total precipitation. This extraordinary feat is accomplished through a complex system of irrigation dams, *wadi* (dry watercourse that becomes a river during the rainy season) diversion channels, aqueducts (under- and above ground), terraced fields, hillside water harvesting channels and cisterns. These ancient systems of water conservation have continued into the modern era.

32. In 1976 the state implemented 1,877 largely rural projects and the LDAs built 6,366. In 1981 the state construction of roads, schools and water projects numbered 4,507 and LDAs built more than 20,000. In 1986 state-sponsored projects totalled 7,821 and LDA projects 23,344 (Carapico 1998, p113).
33. Carapico (1998), pp116-118.
34. ROY *et al*, *Children and Women in Yemen: A Situation Analysis 1998*, Vol I, p13.
35. *Ibid.*

Although currently at risk for a number of reasons, these traditions can continue to provide water to rural communities and households.

Green practices

Traditional building techniques in Yemen are environmentally appropriate to the various climatic regions of the country and provide aesthetically pleasing living spaces. Both urban and rural traditions maximise valuable farmland by constructing multi-storey homes on rocky mountaintops. Stone, mud brick and earth are used to insulate homes from heat and cold. Although skilled craftsmen supervise construction of grander homes and monuments, traditionally most men had building experience and community cooperation in building homes was common. Damaged mud buildings that fell into disrepair melted back into the earth and the stones from masonry structures were salvaged for re-use.

In San'a' the more than 40 traditional gardens have been a model of interdependence and conservation of resources for generations. Traditionally, urban homes separated liquid and solid waste in bathrooms, with faecal matter collected at the bottom of long-drop chutes on the outside of buildings. In the arid mountain climate this dried rapidly and was periodically gathered and taken to the local bathhouse (*hammam*), where it provided fuel for heating the bath water. The resulting ash was then used to fertilise the city's public gardens. At the same time, the wastewater from both the *hammams* and from ablutions (ritual washing before prayer) in the mosque was channelled into the gardens to irrigate crops and trees. This is yet another example of Yemeni traditions which conserve resources with minimal damage to the environment.

Female leadership

Whether or not the Queen of Sheba actually ruled in Yemen, evidence from inscriptions, statues and artefacts indicates that women in ancient South Arabia had important roles as officials, priestesses and businesswomen.[36] Two women shared power with their husbands and ruled in their own name during the 11th and 12th centuries AD. Queen Asma al-Sulayhiyya (1066-1074 AD) and her daughter-in-law Queen 'Arwa (1074-1138 AD) were rulers of the Sulayhid dynasty (1038-1138 AD) and the only two queens in Arab Muslim history to have had the Friday *khutbah* (similar to the Sunday Christian sermon) pronounced in their name. The Yemeni subjects of these queens affectionately called them Bilquis *al-Saghir* (the little Queen of Sheba), as well as *al-Hurra* (meaning a sovereign woman). Female leaders, patrons of public works, scholars, saints and poetesses have figured in Yemeni history. Their career path was never smooth, but these public models of female leadership clearly stem from indigenous traditions that empower women through their productive and reproductive roles. Despite rural women's heavy reproductive and productive responsibilities, there are women in most rural Yemeni communities actively participating in community life.[37] While Yemeni women clearly struggle with inequality (see Chapter V, section 4) they benefit from such positive role models and the historical acceptance of women in positions of leadership.

36. Warburton (1995), p23 and 33.
37. This paragraph is based on information from Mernissi (1993) and Sadek (1993).

Grinding grain, Jabal Raymah, west of Bayt al-Faqih.

MARTA COLBURN

Diversity and tolerance

Yemen is home to diverse regional, social, political, ethnic, linguistic and religious traditions. This pluralism originates from a myriad of sources including location, climate, history and social and economic factors. Domestic and community cultures have been shaped by the lifestyles of fisherfolk, traders, craftspeople, nomads, farmers and pastoralists. Other differences have arisen from the blending of Arab culture and ethnicity with African, Indian, South East Asian and Turkic peoples. Another source of Yemeni diversity is religion. Both Jewish and Christian kingdoms ruled different parts of the country.[38] Today, the vast majority of Yemenis are Muslims, either following the Shi'ah Zaydi or Sunni Shafi'i[39] schools of jurisprudence, with a few Isma'ili communities scattered in the countryside.[40] Sufi traditions are common among Shafi'is.[41] Yemen's diverse religious and ethnic traditions generally illustrate a history of tolerance and cooperation between communities. As G Wyman Bury wrote in the early 20th century 'The Yameni is not fanatical. He has his own religious views, but realizes, from the sects into which his own people are divided, that there are at least two sides to every religious question.'[42]

38. The Axumite Ethiopian Kingdom was Christian during its brief occupations of Yemen in 340 AD and again in 525 AD. During the last few centuries of the Himyarite Kingdom (115 BC-525 AD) various rulers converted to Christianity and then to Judaism (Stookey, 1978, pp18-21).
39. This doctrinal school of Islam is one of the four Sunni (Orthodox) schools of Islamic jurisprudence that first appeared in the central highlands of Yemen in 912-13 and by the end of the Rasulid dynasty in Yemen (1229-1454 AD) Shafi'i Islam was permanently established as the dominant tradition in the southern highlands, coastal areas and most of the former PDRY. (Burrowes, 1995)

40. Isma'ilis are a secretive esoteric branch of Shi'ah Islam that advocates the imamate of a descendant of Isma'il bin Ja'far al-Sadiq. Isma'ili influence in Yemen was widespread from the mid-10th to the mid-11th centuries, when the Sulayhid Dynasty ruled much of the country. (*Ibid.* p195)
41. A term denoting devotees of various mystical brands of Islam which developed from the 7th century AD. In Yemen Sufis find expression among Shafi'is. It is reputed that Yemeni Sufi mystics introduced both *qat* and coffee for human consumption.
42. Bury (1915/1998) p149.

III FOREIGN RELATIONS

The Cold War and international relations before unification

The south western corner of the Arabian Peninsula was largely peripheral to international events in the 20th century. Nevertheless, Yemen was influenced by Cold War and Sino-Soviet competition in a variety of ways. The civil war that followed independence in the YAR represented the height of Cold War tensions in Yemen. During this conflict Egypt and the Soviet Union supported the republican cause, whereas Saudi Arabia and the United Kingdom backed the royalists. Although the United States was one of the first nations to recognise the new republic, during the civil war its 'special relationship' with Saudi Arabia resulted in US support for the royalist cause through arms and military training.

At the conclusion of the civil war in 1970 the YAR's unregulated economy, conservative tribal power base, and non-alignment on many international issues resulted in generally positive foreign relations. YAR leaders proved adept at working both sides of the Cold War to extract material assistance. As one scholar noted, 'Virtually every global, bilateral, and Middle Eastern donor, regardless of ideology, contributed to a level of official development assistance which rose to well over a billion dollars a year around 1980. After that, it fell to about half a billion dollars a year in 1985 and less than [US]$100 million in 1998.'[43]

Socialism was the ideological framework of the PDRY, and the government attempted to maintain good relations with both the Chinese and the Soviets. As the only Marxist Arab country, its policies (such as nationalising the economy and private property, and publicly granting political asylum to various left-wing

43. Carapico (1998) p43.

---

3. COLD WAR ROAD RACE

An early manifestation of Cold War dynamics in the YAR was a race between the United States, the Soviet Union and the People's Republic of China, for each to construct a highway on its allotted side of the San'a'-Ta'izz-Hodeidah triangle. The Chinese began construction in 1961 and continued throughout much of the civil war. The hardworking Chinese labourers were so well liked by the Yemenis that they were never attacked. In this competition, China was clearly the winner, completing the greatly admired 'Chinese Road' connecting San'a' with al-Hodeidah. The United States was clearly the loser – despite the engineering feat of scaling the Yislah (2,600m) and Samara (2,800m) passes – as it refused to pave the road connecting San'a', Ta'izz and Mokha. Its gravelled surface gained the ire of lorry drivers and government officials until it was paved a few years later.

Burrowes, Robert D (1995) *Historical Dictionary of Yemen*, The Scarecrow Press, Inc, London, p118 and Halliday, Fred (1974) *Arabia Without Sultans*, p156.

'terrorist' groups) alienated many in the international community. Thus from 1969 to 1990, the United States labelled the PDRY a 'pariah' state and US citizens were banned from travelling there.

Despite contrasting ideologies and political systems, the Soviet Union was the primary arms supplier for both North and South Yemen. East Germany and Iraq trained and equipped the police and security personnel of both the YAR and the PDRY. North Yemen was among the first Arab countries to recognise the People's Republic of China (PRC) and both Yemens maintained good relations with China, which provided various forms of development assistance. During the 1970s France was one of the few western countries to provide development assistance to the PDRY. Given Cold War dynamics, the numerous conflicts between the YAR and PDRY in the 1970s could have escalated, but did not, owing to economic, social and political (domestic and international) constraints.

Historically the Hijaz (the central and western region of the Arabian Peninsula along the Red Sea coast) and Yemen have had strong ties of trade and faith and there is today a significant community of Saudi citizens of Hadhrami ancestry. Since its establishment in 1932[44] and the increasing importance of oil in the global economy, the Kingdom of Saudi Arabia has become the most powerful regional actor with considerable interests and influence over its impoverished southern neighbours. Saudi-Yemeni relations have rarely been smooth. Tensions have arisen as a result of:

- cultural and religious differences;[45]
- contrasting political systems – monarchy in Saudi Arabia, republican regimes in the Yemens;
- conflict over borders and resources;
- tensions arising from the client-patron relations that developed between Saudi Arabia and both the YAR and the PDRY from the 1970s until the Gulf War;[46]
- until the Gulf War, the hundreds of thousands of Yemeni migrant workers in Saudi Arabia were often a domestic political concern;[47]
- Saudi support for conservative Islamic groups in Yemen, interference in domestic politics and covert assistance to tribal leaders in the northern highlands.

The United States had established diplomatic relations with Imam Yahya in 1946. However, its policy towards Yemen has largely been filtered through its global and regional commitments, particularly its 'special relationship' with Saudi Arabia. This meant that during the civil war in YAR, the United States, via Saudi Arabia, armed and trained royalists while at the same time recognising the republicans. From 1967 to 1972 the YAR suspended diplomatic relations with the

44. 'Abdul 'Aziz ibn Saud proclaimed himself king of the Hijaz and named the country Saudi Arabia.
45. Shaykh Mohammed ibn al-Wahhab (1703-1792) founded a puritanical variant of Islam that opposed the excessive veneration of the Prophet Mohammed and holy places (such as tombs of pious individuals) with a strict adherence to Islamic criminal punishments (such as beheadings, stonings and amputations). An early example of Wahhabi-Yemeni tensions was the 1809 incursion of Wahhabis into the Wadi Hadhramaut where they destroyed tombs and printed materials and then retreated [Halliday (1975) p60].

46. Saudi development assistance to the governments of the YAR and PDRY began in 1973 and 1977, respectively.
47. The 1934 Ta'if Agreement provided for preferential treatment of Yemeni migrant labourers above all other nationalities. During the 1960s and 1970s as the Saudi economy required increasing numbers of guest workers, Muslims were preferred and impoverished Yemenis were a natural choice. However, after Yemenis were implicated in the 1979 attack on the Grand Mosque in Mecca, other nationalities were considered cheaper and less risky [Wenner (1991) p167]

United States owing to the latter's support for Israel in the 1967 Arab-Israeli war. And in the 1979 war between the YAR and PDRY, the United States sold a substantial quantity of arms to the YAR that were paid for by Saudi Arabia. US President Jimmy Carter pushed the transaction through by phrasing it in Cold War terms, but Saudi control of the transfer weakened US-Yemeni relations. During the 1980s relations between the YAR and the United States gradually warmed, with Vice President George Bush visiting in 1986. This was followed by a visit to the United States in 1990 by President 'Ali 'Abdullah Saleh.

Post-independence relations between the two Yemeni states and Britain were shaped by the colonial experience, regional events and global dynamics. In the early years of the PDRY, the recent liberation struggle, economic challenges and continuing financial negotiations with the British left little room for positive interaction.[48] Despite the hostility, commercial relations between the two countries continued until unification in 1990. Whitehall appointed its first ambassador to Aden in 1983. In 1973 the British Council opened for business in the YAR and until 1999 operated high-quality English language instruction for thousands of Yemeni students. In the 1980s British relations with the YAR were relatively smooth and the Overseas Development Administration provided significant support to development projects.

At many points during the republican era altercations arose between Yemen and neighbouring countries. Contentious issues included ill-defined borders inherited from the colonial era, as well as political and ideological conflicts. Relations between Oman and the PDRY were tense during the 1970s and early 1980s owing to PDRY support for the Popular Front for the Liberation of Oman (PFLO) and the Dhufar rebellion (the Omani region bordering Mahra) which waged war against the Sultanate of Oman from 1965 to 1976.[49] Among the more amicable regional relations was that between the Yemens and Kuwait, which until 1990 generously contributed to human development in both the PDRY and YAR. In 1984, His Excellency Shaykh Zayid B Sultan al-Nahayan, the former oil minister of the United Arab Emirates, funded a new Ma'rib dam. Shaykh Zayid and other Gulf Arabs believe they are descended from Yemenis who emigrated from the region when the Ma'rib dam burst in the 6th century AD.

At the end of the 1980s numerous key developments affected Yemeni foreign relations. As a result of perestroika and growing economic and political challenges, the Soviet Union dramatically reduced foreign assistance, financial support and trade with the YAR and PDRY. Assistance from Saudi Arabia, Kuwait and other oil-rich Arab states also diminished as their economies slowed. Migrant labour and remittances had begun to decline in the mid-1980s. Although oil was discovered in modest quantities in the YAR and PDRY in the 1980s, revenue was slow to materialise and was unable to compensate for the loss of other sources of income.

The idea of Yemeni unity was highly popular, particularly after the YAR revolution in 1962. However, when the PDRY proclaimed independence in 1967, neither country was capable of serious steps to realise this goal. In fact, tensions between the two regimes erupted in border clashes of varying intensity in 1971, 1972, 1978, 1979 and 1988. Nevertheless, throughout the republican era the rhetoric of unity remained consistent and in the 1980s steps were taken to clarify key issues. In 1989 the YAR and the PDRY agreed to unite and declared the Republic of Yemen on 22 May. Domestic political, economic and social factors contributed to unity in 1990, as did global developments such as the collapse of the former Soviet

48. Before independence the United Kingdom had promised £60 million, and another £12 million at the Geneva independence negotiations. In the end, it paid £1.25 million. At the British departure 35,000 jobs were lost and independence coincided with the closing of the Suez Canal during the 1967 Arab-Israeli war. [Lackner (1985), p53 and 57].
49. Burrowes (1995) p132.

Union and the end of the Cold War. However, unification (or 'reunification' as many Yemenis preferred to call it) proceeded only because of commitments to power-sharing, multi-party democracy and economic and social liberalisation.

The Gulf War

On 2 August 1990, a little over two months after Yemeni unification, Iraq invaded Kuwait. The resulting Gulf War was a watershed in Yemen's foreign relations, and had a far-reaching impact on domestic affairs. As the only Arab country on the UN Security Council in 1990-91, Yemen's position of neutrality and advocacy of a non-military Arab diplomatic solution, was seen as *de facto* support for Saddam Hussein by Kuwait, Saudi Arabia, many other Arab countries, and the United States. As a result Saudi Arabia, Kuwait and the Gulf states cut off their substantial financial assistance to Yemen, including a US$300 million aid package from Saudi Arabia and Kuwait alone.[50] The US government reduced its assistance programme from US$42 million a year to US$3million.[51]

---

4. AN EXPENSIVE VOTE

In 1990 the ROY abstained from voting on UN Security Council Resolutions 660 and 661 which condemned Iraq's invasion of Kuwait, called for its immediate and unconditional withdrawal, and imposed economic sanctions. Yemen also voted against Resolution 678 (allowing member states to use all necessary means to implement Resolution 660 and all subsequent relevant resolutions). Following the vote on 678 a senior US official informed the ROY delegate that it would be the most expensive 'no' vote Yemen had ever cast.

Burrowes (1995) and Middle East Watch (1992).

At the same time, between 800,000 and 1 million Yemeni workers were expelled from Saudi Arabia and the Gulf.[52] These individuals were largely unskilled labourers (almost half were illiterate with only 18 per cent having any formal education) who returned during the worst drought in years, with limited assets, disconnected from tribal, village or family systems of support.[53] Many were forced to settle in shanty towns outside Aden and Hodeidah, and in 'earthquake housing' constructed outside Dhamar city following the 1982 earthquake.[54] Workers' remittances had declined steadily from a high of nearly US$2 billion annually in the late 1970s and early 1980s to US$300 million in the early 1990s.[55]

---

50. Human Rights Watch/Middle East (1992) p2.
51. US State Department (1996).
52. 'This amounted to double punishment of Yemen, for not only did the country suffer a sudden loss of remittances but also faced the problem of absorbing this huge influx of returnees. In the space of three months, Yemen experienced a 7 per cent increase in its population and a 15 per cent increase in its workforce, severely exacerbating unemployment. To begin to comprehend the upheaval this caused, in proportional terms one would have to imagine close to four million British expatriate suddenly arriving at Dover – jobless and largely homeless.' (Whitaker, 2000b)
53. Many Yemeni migrant labourers had been away from their home villages since the 1970s when massive waves of out-migration to Saudi Arabia and the Gulf began.
54. This earthquake registered 6.2 on the Richter scale and its epicentre was in Dhawran Anis, a small village in the western highlands of Dhamar governorate. It killed over 1,500 people, levelled whole villages and left an estimated 400,000 homeless.
55. Al-Maitami (1998a) p2.

Post-unification

The Gulf War altered key foreign relations of the ROY. Saudi-Yemeni relations did not begin to thaw until 1992-93, although tensions escalated again with the 1994 Yemeni civil war.[56] US-Yemeni relations had been damaged severely and although many in the US State Department were urging a more supportive policy towards Yemen, others remembered the 1990 position of neutrality. Yemen's critical economic situation and deteriorating relations between the former YAR and PDRY leaders provided ample opportunity for opponents of unity. The separatists found a ready ally in Saudi Arabia (and possibly Kuwait). Opponents of unity were clearly the losers in the conflict and Saudi-Yemeni relations deteriorated to levels not seen since the 1960s royalist-republican war. By 2000, however, Saudi domestic politics had changed dramatically, which affected its policy towards Yemen. The Jiddah Treaty of 2000 between the two countries resolved their long-standing border dispute and relations improved. The treaty included agreement on:

- fixed land and maritime co-ordinates with a grid reference demarcating the provisional land boundary well to the north of borders previously claimed by Saudi Arabia;
- an independent survey to connect the fixed positions;
- promotion of commercial, economic and cultural relations;
- cooperation in the event of 'shared natural wealth';
- agreement on mutual non-interference in domestic affairs.

Yemenis frequently assert that the Saudis interfere covertly in Yemeni domestic affairs by paying 'cooperative' tribal leaders, bankrolling tribal lawlessness and even buying votes.[57] It is interesting that the incidence of kidnapping has decreased dramatically since the signing of the treaty, with only three cases in 2000 after the treaty was signed and seven in 2001, compared with 10 in 1999, 11 in 1998 and 10 in 1997.

While Yemen's relations with Saudi Arabia in the 1990s were fraught with tension, relations with Oman have steadily improved. In 1992 a border agreement was negotiated with Oman; the final map was approved in 1995. This treaty normalised relations, signalling a new era of cooperation between two modern countries that have had strong connections for more than 1,500 years.

Another regional relationship of importance in the mid-1990s was with Eritrea. In December 1995 Eritrean forces occupied Greater Hanish Island, one of three larger islands in an archipelago in the Red Sea approximately half-way between the two countries. The two governments subsequently agreed to international legal arbitration. In 1998 and 1999 the Permanent Court of Arbitration at The Hague ruled in favour of Yemen.

Yemen's foreign relations in this period were also affected by the kidnapping in December 1998 of a group of 16 tourists by Islamic extremists from the Aden-Abyan Islamic Army. The government rescue attempt the following day resulted in the deaths of three Britons and one Australian. The subsequent arrest and trial of eight British citizens and two Algerians believed to be connected to the kidnapping created significant tensions between Yemen and Britain. The situation was exacerbated by Yemeni accusations that a radical Britain-based Muslim cleric, Abu Hamza, was responsible for instigating this and other terrorist

56. The conflict of 1994 between elements of the former PDRY and other post-unification leaders has been variously referred to as a civil war, a war of secession or an attempted coup d'etat. Here, it will be referred to as the 1994 civil war.
57. 'During the 1991 constitutional referendum, the men of Sa'ada in the far north were allegedly bribed to abstain from voting but defied the Saudis by sending their wives to vote instead.' This claim is substantiated by the fact that Sa'ada, a traditionally conservative area, had the highest female voter turnout in the country (including Aden). (Whitaker 2000b)

activity in Yemen. Rising tensions eventually led to the cessation of English language teaching at the British Council. Both the United States and Britain issued travel warnings against non-essential travel to Yemen.

In June 1999, Yemen hosted an international conference 'Emerging Democracies Forum: Managing the Twin Transitions: Political and Economic Reform' with delegations from 16 countries undergoing democratisation (including Namibia and El Salvador, where CIIR/ICD has programmes). Sponsored by the Yemeni government with assistance from the international donor community, this event demonstrated Yemen's commitment to democratisation and earned international recognition for its leadership. In many ways the conference reflected key commitments of Yemeni foreign policy in the 1990s, characterised by non-alignment and the search for negotiated solutions to inter-Arab and regional conflicts.

Doorway
Hajjarah

ADAM BRADBURY/CIIR-ICD

MARTA COLBURN

Ochre-painted mud brick architecture in Baradh mountains, north of San'a'.

Houses, Hajjarah

San'a'

Wall decorations, Hajjarah

ADAM BRADBURY/CIIR-ICD

DINNY HAWES/CIIR-ICD

Terracing, Jabin. Terracing on the highest mountains in designed to retain water and release it in a controlled flow.

Cistern outside the walled city of Hajjarah, near Manakha, southwest San'a' Governorate.

BRUCE PALUCK

DINNY HAWES/CIIR-ICD

Oola, Reymah

DINNY HAWES/CIIR-ICD

The old city, San'a'

DINNY HAWES/CIIR-ICD

Rainbow over Jabin and Bayt Al Sheik

BRUCE PALUCK

Bab al-Yemen (the Gate of Yemen), the entrance to the old city of San'a' built by the Ottoman Turks at the beginning of the 20th century.

DINNY HAWES/CIIR-ICD

Threshing millet, Tihamah.

Threshing grains on road to KawKaban, northwest of San'a'.

DONALD COLBURN

MARTA COLBURN

Woman carrying animal fodder, Jabal Raymah, west of Bayt al-Faqih.

JUDITH GARDNER/CIIR-ICD

Money changer, San'a.

Camel train carrying wood for fuel up into the mountains, Al Jabin.

DINNY HAWES/CIIR-ICD

Despite political advances for women, literacy rates remain low — 35 per cent in 1998 compared to 69 per cent of men.

ADAM BRADBURY/CIIR-ICD

Imported dates sold in the market near Hajjarah.

PIPPA HOYLAND/CIIR-ICD

Health education message explaining the importance of a good diet in pregnancy. Only 30 per cent of Yemen's population has access to adequate health care. Government reform of health care has included limited cost-recovery programmes.

Terracing north of San'a'.

Qasmi traditional garden (maqshama) in the old city of San'a' (see page 25).

MARTA COLBURN

Grinding henna leaves in Jabal Raymah, west of Bayt al-Faqih.

Wedding dance in an Eritrean refugee camp in Khokha, Tihamah Governorate.

Traditional judge at Wadi Phahr, northwest of San a .

Farming couple with banana and papaya trees in an experimental farm on the Tihamah.

Young girl with her hair decorated with jasmine buds, red antimony and sweet-smelling spices at a wedding in 'Abs, Northern Tihamah Governorate.

MARTA COLBURN

Decorations inside a house in the Tihamah

DINNY HAWES/CIIR-ICD

MARTA COLBURN

Driving through the city of 'Amran after a rainstorm, northwest of San'a'.

IV DEVELOPMENT CHALLENGES TODAY

Entering the 21st century, 76 per cent of Yemen's population still live in communities of fewer than 500 residents, exacerbating problems of service delivery by an inefficient and often corrupt government bureaucracy. More than 50 per cent of Yemen's estimated population of 18.7 million are under the age of 15. With an annual growth rate of 3.4 per cent (among the highest in the world) the population is projected to double in the next 20 years. The pre-unification pattern of high security and defence budgets and low spending on health care and education has continued into the ROY era. A decade after unification, the ROY is ranked 148th (out of 174 countries) on the UN Human Development Index.

1. The 1990s: Economic crisis and reform

Yemen's economy inherited certain characteristics and government practices from the YAR and PDRY eras that have constrained efforts at human and economic development. The post-unification economy has also been deeply affected by political and social crises. Although the government initiated an economic reform process in 1995, the reforms have yet to prove effective and their long-term impact on Yemeni citizens is unclear.

Systemic limitations

Since ancient times Yemen's economy has been agrarian. A primary concern for the ROY is low agricultural productivity. The sector employs nearly 60 per cent of Yemenis, but in 1999 it contributed only 16 per cent to the GDP (excluding *qat* [58] production). The reasons for low productivity include:

- water scarcity;
- lack of resources and coordination for maintaining traditional rainwater diversion structures;
- lack of infrastructure for transporting, preserving and processing agricultural products;
- insufficient and inappropriate extension services;
- deterioration of traditional terraces and loss of top-soil, particularly during the years of high labour out-migration; and
- lack of research on appropriate ways to enhance agricultural production.

One result of low agricultural productivity is that Yemen imports approximately 75 per cent of the cereal it consumes.[59] This dependency could jeopardise food security, particularly given rapid population growth, a negative balance of payments and foreign currency shortages.

   Yemen has a substantial informal sector, estimated to be nearly as large as the

58. A shrub whose leaves are chewed to produce a mildly stimulating euphoric sensation.
59. World Bank (1999), p16.

5. A SNAPSHOT OF DEVELOPMENT CHALLENGES IN THE NEW MILLENNIUM

- In 1997 Yemeni women aged 15-49 years had a total **fertility** rate of 6.5 live children, with an urban rate of 6.25 and a rural rate of nearly eight (one of the highest fertility rates in the world and more than double the world average).

- In 1998 female **life expectancy** was 61 years (urban 62.6 and rural 59.6) and male was 57.5 (urban 58.5 and rural 56.6) – one of the smallest gender gaps in the world.

- In 1998 **infant mortality** was estimated to be 87/1,000 and under-five mortality 121/1,000 (compared to the Middle East regional average of 46 to 60 out of 1,000).

- **Maternal mortality** rates mean that Yemeni women face a one in eight chance of dying of pregnancy-related causes.

- Only 30 per cent of Yemen's rural population has access to adequate **health services** and household out-of-pocket contributions to health care are 91 per cent of the total cost for services.

- It is estimated that only 60 per cent of urban households are connected to **drinking water systems** (not necessarily potable) and fewer than half of rural households have access to potable water (compared to the regional average of 82 per cent). Only 19 per cent of households nationwide are connected to sanitation or sewage systems.

- Yemen has a scarcity of **arable land**; only 2.9 per cent (1.6 million hectares) of the country is prime farmland, with another 3.7 per cent (2 million hectares) being marginal farmland.

- In 1998 the national **illiteracy rate** was 47 per cent, 31 per cent for males and 64 per cent for females. Urban rates were 30 per cent total, 21 per cent male and 39 per cent female, and rural rates 54 per cent total, 35 per cent male and 73 per cent female.

- Less than 80 per cent of eligible six- to nine-year-old children are enrolled in **basic education** (only 55 per cent of eligible girls) and of those enrolled less than 45 per cent of girls and only 66 per cent of boys reach the eighth grade.

- Since the 1960s Yemen's urban population has grown from approximately 10 per cent to 25 per cent of the country's total (1994 census), with the city of San'a' expanding at an annual rate of 11 per cent and thus tripling in the 1990s. This **urbanisation** has contributed to the growth of urban shantytowns, overcrowded classrooms (the average classroom in San'a' has 90 students) and overstretched services.

Information in this section is based on data from World Bank (1997) *Yemen: Towards a Water Strategy*, ROY et al, *Children and Women in Yemen: A Situation Analysis* (1998) and ROY (2000) *Government Interim Poverty Reduction Strategy Paper*.

60. Nonneman (1995), p1.

61. According to the *Yemen Observer*, 'Smuggled cigarettes account for 15 per cent to 25 per cent of the Yemeni market, smuggled foodstuffs account for 29 per cent to 35 per cent, smuggled biscuits and chocolates for 30 per cent-45 per cent. About 75 per cent of medicine is smuggled into Yemen.' (1 October 1999)

formal economy.[60] While producers in the informal sector have advantages (such as exemption for taxes and other forms of government interference), this complicates government planning and policy development. Moreover, the sector falls outside government regulation of workers' benefits, rights and protection. This is of particular significance for marginalised groups, such as women, refugees and undocumented immigrants who work in the informal sector.

National integration of the economy is weak, as a result of inadequate roads, electricity, water supply and communications. Distribution problems between regions are exacerbated by central government's lack of economic control. Smuggling in and out of Yemen is a serious problem. Weapons, consumer goods, alcohol and medicine are easily smuggled in by sea and land across borders that present limited barriers to ingenuity and bribery.[61] Smugglers can easily transport *qat*, arms, drugs and government-subsidised goods (in particular, petrol and grains) to Yemen's neighbours. Smuggling deprives the government of customs revenue, creates unfair competition for locally produced goods and contributes to corruption of government officials.

Government practice

At unification the new state inherited a national debt of US$5.8 billion (US$3.3 billion from the YAR and US$2.5 billion from the PDRY), of which 45 per cent was owed to Russia (primarily for military equipment). By 1996 the national debt had reached US$8 billion, 1.5 times the GDP. However, in a series of gatherings the World Bank (WB) and various donor countries, including Russia, worked out a system to reduce the debt by rescheduling loans at improved rates and outright cancellation. Yemen's total debt to Russia of US$5.8 billion was reduced by US$5 billion. By the end of 2000, Yemen's foreign debt had dropped to US$2.5 billion.[62]

High government spending on the military has reduced expenditure for essential services. Yemen's armed forces are estimated at nearly 110,000 soldiers with 75,000 reservists and an unknown number of security personnel. In July 2000 the Minister of Planning and Development, Ahmed Sufan, stated that Yemen's annual military spending between 1997 and 1998 had consumed up to 15 per cent of Yemen's GDP and more than 32 per cent of the state budget.[63] This enormous expenditure on the military is in stark contrast to the low levels of government spending on health care (2.1 per cent in 1996-98) and on education (7 per cent in 1995-97).[64]

Other legacies from the YAR and PDRY are deficits in balance of payments, trade and the national budget.[65] Since the height of the remittance boom in the late 1970s and early 1980s, both North and South Yemen imported more than they exported. From 1990 to 1994 Yemen ran an average balance of payments deficit of nearly US$1 billion annually. The governments of both the YAR and the PDRY had budget deficits, a pattern continued in the ROY. In the early 1990s the

62. Information about foreign debts is from al-Maitami (1998a) p5 and *Yemen Times* (2000) 29 May 29-4 June.

63. *Yemen Times* (2000) 24-30 July.

64. UNDP (2000) p216.

65. Balance of payments deficits averaged well above US$1 billion annually during the early 1990s.

---

6. A DECADE OF CONSUMER PROTEST

1991 – in October young men in six towns demonstrated over the deteriorating economic system.

1992 – in December, 60 people were killed, hundreds injured and thousands detained by police in urban protests against the government and merchants. Demonstrations became riots when police fired on crowds in San'a'. Reportedly thousands of people in Ta'izz participated in burning and looting.

1995 – in March a reduction of subsidies on petrol, cooking gas and electricity led to demonstrations which were particularly violent in Aden.

1996 – in January currency devaluations and reduction of subsidies pushed up prices (wheat and flour by 150 per cent, petrol by 64 per cent, kerosene by 200 per cent, diesel by 100 per cent and cooking gas by 100 per cent). This led to demonstrations in Aden and Dhamar and farmers blocked the main road to San'a'.

1997 – in October diesel fuel prices rose by more than 30 per cent and kerosene by 85 per cent. Protests erupted throughout Yemen and farmers in Ma'rib protested by blocking access to oil fields.

1998 – in June demonstrations erupted in all major urban areas in the north when the government withdrew subsidies (petrol prices rose by 40 per cent, wheat and flour by 35 per cent, cooking gas by 25 per cent). Fifty-two people were killed and hundreds wounded in the unrest.

Based on Carapico (1996) and (1998) and various *Yemen Times* articles at the time of the protests.

ROY budget deficits were running at between 20 and 30 per cent of annual GDP[66] and were sustained by issuing banknotes and borrowing. The economic reform process launched in 1995 addressed these issues by reducing expenditures on social services and increasing income from taxes and oil thus contributing to the deteriorating situation of the middle class and the poor.

Post-unification patterns

After unification the expansion of the cash crop *qat* became an important economic concern. Its spread has been particularly dramatic in the south, where under the PDRY *qat* usage had been strictly limited to weekends and holidays. It is estimated that *qat* contributes 25 per cent of Yemen's GDP and 16 per cent of employment, but consumes 30 per cent of its water.[67] *Qat* production exploded from 8,000 hectares in 1970, to 77,000 in 1990 and 91,000 in 1996, and contributed significantly to Yemen's groundwater overdraft.[68] A cash crop that has often been proposed as a solution to the *qat* problem is coffee. Although the production and profitability of this crop have decreased from the days of the Yemeni monopoly in the , production gradually increased in the 1990s and profits have increased dramatically (by 190 per cent between 1993 and 1998).[69]

Land tenure in Yemen is diverse and often unrecorded. However, research has demonstrated that there is a trend towards increasing fragmentation of holdings, as well as more sharecropping. The majority of farms are divided into small plots: some 20 per cent are less than two hectares, 24 per cent are between two and five hectares, and 56 per cent are between five and 50 hectares.[70] With unification, large tracts of land that had been nationalised and farmed cooperatively under the PDRY were returned to original owners, including many Sultans from the British colonial era. Most former members of cooperative farms, including many women, are now wage labourers. The World Bank estimates that approximately 76 per cent of land in the northern highlands is owner-occupied, and another 11 per cent is owned and operated by absentee landlords.[71]

Throughout the 1990s tourism was an important source of foreign currency as well as employment. Between 1988 and 1997, revenues from tourism ranged from a low of US$19 million in 1994 to US$69 million in 1997. However, in 1998 the incidence of kidnapping increased and an estimated US$28 million in revenue from tourism was lost in the first half of the year.[72] The kidnapping and killing of tourists in December 1998 further reduced this source of revenue as many western governments issued travel warnings urging their citizens to avoid non-essential travel to Yemen. Although there was a modest increase in tourism in 2000 and 2001 the sector is clearly highly sensitive to domestic and international events.

A further economic challenge is the heavy reliance on the petroleum sector, which generates 93 per cent of export income and 70 per cent of government revenues. The over-reliance on oil was particularly apparent when the Asian economic crisis struck (76 per cent of Yemeni exports go to Asian countries). In 1998 the price of oil dropped; in 1999 the average price per barrel was US$10, the lowest since the mid-1970s. As a result, 1998 oil revenues were down by 30 per cent from 1997 levels and the 1998 budget deficit rose by 13 per cent. The price recovered to US$30 per barrel by April 2001. Oil, however, is a sensitive and finite resource. Development of Yemen's natural gas reserves, estimated at 13-15 trillion cubic feet, has been slow because of the Asian economic crisis. However, in the

66. Nonneman (1995) p8.
67. World Bank (1997) p5.
68. World Bank (1999) p2.
69. In 1970 approximately 7,000 hectares (World Bank 1993, p18) were cultivated in coffee, rising to 24,500 hectares producing 8,700 tons in 1993 and more than 32,000 hectares, producing 11,300 tons, in 1998 (CSO 1998, pp41-44).
70. World Bank (1997) p36.
71. World Bank (1993) p1.
72. *Yemen Times* 13-19 July 1998.

early years of the 21st century gas is expected to begin yielding revenues that will offset decreasing petroleum earnings.

In the post-unification period in the wake of the Gulf War, the ROY faced tough political and economic challenges. The expense of unifying two diverse economies, military establishments and government bureaucracies was considerable. Democratisation required funding for various institutions, such as the Supreme Election Committee and Parliament, as well as voter registration and election polling. While some assistance was made available to the ROY (for example, the Libyan housing complex built next to San'a' University intended for the southern leadership) much of it was suspended or terminated by the Gulf War.

The 1994 civil war also had a significant economic impact. The 70-day conflict resulted in an estimated 6,000 civilian and military wounded and 1,500 dead. Estimates of the war's material cost range from US$7 million[73] to US$13 million.[74]

Economic reform

Economic decline led the ROY government in 1995 to embark on economic and structural reforms, with the assistance of the World Bank, the International Monetary Fund (IMF) and the international donor community. The initial reforms were designed to free interest rates, adjust foreign exchange rates and liberalise trade. In 1996 the IMF approved a credit and loan package totalling US$512 million for 1997-2000, in support of Yemen's Structural Adjustment Programme. This was designed to:

- reorient support to social services and public investment in infrastructure;
- increase government revenue from taxation;
- eliminate subsidies;
- initiate civil service, pension fund, customs administration and budgetary management reforms;
- implement financial sector reforms focusing on indirect monetary control, improvement of the banking system, privatisation and enhanced competitiveness.

73. Nonneman (1995) p8.
74. Al-Maitami (1998a) p3.

Table 4. The economy in the 1990s

Indicator	1990	1992	1994	1996	1998
Average annual exchange rate Yemeni Rials = US$1	13.92	28.50	55.24	128	135.88
Per Capita GNP	$701	$452	$321	$282	$275
GDP at market price ($ billion)*	8.890	6.413	4.865	5.118	5.160
Inflation	35%	55%	75% 145% unofficial	29%	11%
External debt ($ billions)**	9.9	9.6	8.8	8	4.9
Oil production (barrels per day)	182,000	182,000	335,000	360,000	409,000 (1999)
Exports ($ millions)***.	1,400	950	1,800	1,700	1,300
Imports ($ millions)***	1,900	1,500	2,650	1,500	2,170

Data for this table was gathered from a variety of sources, primarily relying on Al-Maitami (1998a) and the Central Statistical Organization's *1998 Statistical Yearbook*.
*These figures have been calculated in US$ based on ROY government information published in the Central Statistical Organization's *1998 Statistical Yearbook*.
** These debt figures include both long- and short-term debt taken from Gazzo (1999), p327.
***1990-94 from Nonneman (1997) and 1996 and 1998 from the Central Statistical Organization's *1998 Statistical Yearbook*.

The initial phases of the reform process reduced the budget deficit and inflation and boosted GDP growth. According to the IMF:

> The economy responded favourably to these measures, with real non-oil GDP recovering by 7 per cent in 1995 and expanding by 3 per cent in 1996. The budget deficit was reduced from 17 per cent of GDP in 1994 to 2.3 per cent of GDP in 1996. With this tightened fiscal stance supported by firm monetary policies, the core inflation rate (which excludes the effect of

7. THE BITTER PILL OF STRUCTURAL ADJUSTMENT

The unpopularity of economic reform was evident in the 1996 and 1998 consumer demonstrations that ensued followed withdrawal of government subsidies on fuel and basic food items. Demonstrators demanded the resignation of the new government headed by Dr Abdul Karim al-Iryani, a seasoned politician and diplomat. In an interview Dr al-Iryani stated: Reform will never be popular, and if I had some measure of popularity, I would prepare myself to lose it within 24 hours. Those who think that there is a magic stick that will make the bitter remedy sweet, will quickly lose their hope. There is no avoiding severity and there is no evading difficult decisions.

Efforts of Economic Programme and Structural Adjustment by Dr Mohammed al-Maitami at: www.al-bab.com

8. THE 1990s: THE HUMAN COST OF CRISIS AND REFORM

- Per capita GNP plummeted from US$701 in 1990 to US$275 in 1999.
- From 1990 to 1996 the price of a 50-kilo bag of rice rose from 350 Yemeni rials (YR) to 2,000 rials, an increase of 575 per cent.
- Poverty levels doubled between 1992 and 1998, with the proportion of households below the poverty line rising from 19 per cent to 33 per cent. A 1996 World Bank study showed that 81 per cent of all Yemen s poor and 83 per cent of the absolute poor live in rural areas.
- In 1998 unemployment was estimated at 40 per cent, with the highest proportion of those living in the south.
- The once small and stable middle class is slowly but steadily dying out. In 1984, one US dollar purchased four Yemeni rials and the average public school teacher earned about YR 4,000 a month (US$1,000). In 1999, one US dollar purchased around YR 158 and the average teacher earned approximately YR 14,000 a month (less than US$100).
- Between 1990-93 and 1994-96, average real per capita government spending on health care fell by 37 per cent; spending on education dropped by 28 per cent in the same period.
- A small economic elite commands increasing wealth, in contrast to the burgeoning ranks of the poor. By 2000 the poorest 10 per cent of households spent only 3.5 per cent of national income; the richest 10 per cent of households controlled 34 per cent of income in Yemen, and accounted for 25 per cent of expenditure.

Information in this section is based on data from *Children and Women in Yemen: A Situation Analysis* (1998), ROY Government (2000) Interim Poverty Reduction Strategy Paper, Carapico (1998) and the United Nations (2001) *Yemen Common Country Assessment.*

increases in administered prices) fell from 66 per cent in 1994 to 12 per cent in 1996. The overall deficit in the balance of payments declined from 15 per cent of GDP in 1994 to 7 per cent in 1996.[75]

An essential component of these economic reforms has been to establish government- and donor-supported social safety nets and poverty alleviation programmes. This has included policy-level actions such as coordinating the preparation of the Second Five-Year Plan (2001-2005) and to develop a poverty reduction strategy. The government has also taken concrete measures to alleviate poverty, such as the 1996 Social Care Law which provides a small monthly cash payment to the poor and the Productive Family Programme, which provides training primarily to female-headed households. The quasi-governmental Social Fund for Development and the Public Works Project are designed to employ the poor, assist poor communities and target categories of poor such as women and the *akhdam*.[76] To date, the impact of these programmes is still unclear. They have been augmented by World Bank and IMF funding for continuing economic and governmental reform.

2. Challenges for government

The legal and constitutional framework of the ROY demonstrates a commitment to democratisation, the development of civil society and the protection of human rights. Its founding document is the constitution approved by the legislatures of the YAR and PDRY on 21 May 1990. Originally drafted in 1981, this 'unity constitution' was approved by popular referendum in 1991 and amended in 1994 and 2001. The document articulates the founding principles of the Republic, setting forth its political, economic, social, cultural and defence foundations and outlining the roles of democratic legislative, executive and judiciary institutions. It is the framework for legislation, establishes the rights and obligations of citizens and provides procedures for its own amendment.[77]

The ROY is a signatory to many international human rights treaties. In an effort to improve its human rights record, in 1998 the government established the Supreme National Committee for Human Rights to liaise with international human rights organisations and monitor the implementation of human rights treaties. In 1998 the president established the Consultative Council's Human Rights Committee and in April 2001 the new government established the Ministry of Human Rights headed by the first female minister, Dr Wahiba Far'a'. The ROY has allowed international human rights organisations such as Amnesty International and Human Rights Watch to visit and conduct research in the country relatively unhindered. A number of local NGOs working on human rights issues in Yemen are allowed to operate locally, regionally and internationally with minimal government interference. Despite these concrete steps to improve human rights a number of critical issues remain. They include:

- women's rights (see page 65 on gender and development);
- limitations on freedom of speech and freedom of the press;
- constraints on political parties;
- abuses by the security forces;

75. IMF (1997).
76. The *akhdam* (meaning servants) are a group occupying the lowest position in the traditional Yemeni social hierarchy. Although their social status has improved since the 1960s, many continue to work in what are considered dirty jobs, such as street sweeping and garbage collecting.
77. The full text of the ROY Constitution can be viewed on-line at: www.al-bab.com/yemen

9. WATER CRISIS IN AL-SINAH

In the community of al-Sinah, between Ta'izz and Turbah, the women used to have to walk 4.5 miles and carry water nearly 2,000 feet uphill (many villages in Yemen are built on mountain tops for protection and to avoid building on agricultural land). In the 1960s the community decided to develop a piped drinking water system. To pay for it the women in the community sold their gold and villagers working away from home contributed. The scheme was successful, but by 1985 the original wells had dried up. The villagers found a new source near the old wells but the neighbouring village objected because the site was in its territory. The villagers of al-Sinah then found a third water source on land in another district, but owned by members of their community. They made a deal with the neighbouring community and dug deep wells. However, the use of wells for irrigated farming was becoming more common in the area and to protect their last source of drinking water, al-Sinah began to buy land in the area, drill wells and cap them off. This was because communities in the region recognised spacing restrictions of 500-1,000 yards between wells. The capped wells counted, so no one else has drilled near their water source.

World Bank (1997) *Yemen: Towards a Water Strategy.*

- inadequate prison facilities and inhumane treatment of prisoners;
- violations of citizens' legal rights, particularly for citizens from marginalised groups; and
- weakness of the rule of law, enabling powerful individuals and tribes to commit crimes with impunity.[78]

A key issue for the Yemeni government is water. The main factors contributing to Yemen's growing water crisis are: one of the highest population growth rates in the world (3.7% annually); farmers choosing to grow water-intensive cash crops such as *qat*[79]; and the use of new technologies to over-pump groundwater. It is estimated that Yemenis use little more than 150m³ per person per year, compared with the Middle East and North African average of 1,250m³ and the worldwide average of 7,500m³. In many isolated rural areas it is estimated that women spend up to eight hours a day procuring water for their families. This is a task only for younger women, as they must have the strength and endurance to carry a load of water on their heads for great distances. Many towns in Yemen also have severe water supply problems. In 1984 in the San'a' basin, where it is estimated that 10 per cent of the population live, water was being consumed four times as fast as it was being replenished by rain. This groundwater problem exists in most urban areas and rural communities are often located at a considerable distance from a water source. The water shortage is critical not only because of its severity, but also because the government has yet to take measures to address it.

The economic reform programme was accompanied by wide-ranging reforms designed to improve governance. The critical issues here are transparency and accountability, capacity and effectiveness, and the rule of law.

Transparency and accountability

'Transparency' means that stakeholders in public administration can follow the decision-making process and that its criteria, laws and policies have no secret agendas or distortions. The term 'accountability' refers to the ability of citizens,

78. For current human rights information on the internet see: www.hrw.org/; www.amnesty.org/; and www.state.gov/
79. It is estimated that *qat* accounts for 30 per cent of water consumption in Yemen (World Bank, 1997, p5).

creditors and donors to hold the government responsible for its finances and operation. The ROY constitution provides a reasonable legal framework for government transparency and accountability. It establishes standards of ethical behaviour for government officials to prevent 'conflict-of-interest, malfeasance, threats to the national security, administrative violations and a need to disclose financial interests'.[80] Nevertheless, corruption remains a major concern for many in the government, as well as citizens and donors.

Many factors contribute to government corruption. First, the economic crisis has encouraged corruption, as government salaries are inadequate to cover the escalating cost of living (police officers' salaries range from YR6,000 to YR9,000 a month, equivalent to US$37 to US$56).[81] Second, it is difficult to detect and prove corruption charges because financial records in ministries are inadequate and until recently there were no income tax records for employees.[82] Third, corruption is rarely punished. As one journalist pointed out, 'Newspapers and even government agencies such as the Central Organization for Control and Audit report various kinds of abuse, but no action is taken.'[83] Fourth, the political will to confront the issue is lacking. One reason for this is that many government appointments are made on the basis of party, region, tribe, family or patron-client relationship and prosecution of abuses would be construed as targeting the source of the appointment. Finally, government employees who use their position for personal benefit are difficult to prosecute because corruption is perceived to exist up to the highest levels of government.

Capacity and effectiveness

Good governance is compromised by the lack of capacity to operate and deliver basic services. The problems stem from overly complex procedures, lack of communication and coordination within and between ministries, and shortcomings in policy and planning. They are exacerbated by the isolation of rural communities, urbanisation and the population explosion, and the lack of sufficient resources to train, equip and modernise the bureaucracy and provide services.

The over-burdened civil service payroll is another key weakness. A recent study shows that ministries are overstaffed by about 40 per cent. Both pre-unification governments were their countries' major employers, but state payrolls have grown significantly since 1990. Between 1990 and 1995 the government payroll was used as a form of poverty alleviation and the number of employees almost doubled from approximately 170,000 to 320,000.[84] Civil servants' productivity is

80. UNDP (1999) p33.
81. US State Department (2000) p4.
82. *Ibid*, p34.
83. *Yemen Times*, 7-15 February 1999.
84. World Bank (1997) p31.

---

10. THE TRAGEDY OF INADEQUATE HEALTH CARE

At 3am a young woman arrived at the government hospital in labour with a ruptured uterus. Because intravenous needles and bags were not available, the doctor told the husband to go to the pharmacy to buy IVs and antibiotics. The family was poor, and he did not have the money. The doctor gave him the only 100 YR note she had with her. He searched, and after two hours returned with the IVs. Surgery was needed, so he was sent off again to buy the gloves and other supplies required. He returned four hours later. The surgery could begin at 9am. The woman died.

ROY et al, Children and Women in Yemen: A Situation Analysis 1998, Vol. II, p 40.

low and at times salaries go unpaid. Most employees have to hold down two and sometimes three jobs to make ends meet.

Inadequate or intermittent service delivery indicates incapacity and inefficiency in government. Health centres often lack basic supplies and thus cannot deliver essential services. Poor service delivery affects most other government services, including water,[85] electricity, education[86] and road construction and maintenance.

The rule of law

The term 'rule of law' refers to a social, economic and political system in which the laws are clear public knowledge and apply equally to all citizens. Unification largely imposed the legal system of the former YAR, a system which combined elements of *shari'ah* (Islamic or canonical law), *'urf* (customary or tribal law), vestiges of Ottoman codes and Egyptian-patterned commercial, civil and criminal codes. The main challenges facing the Yemeni judiciary are:

- lack of judicial independence;
- inappropriate and insufficient education and skills of legal and administrative staff;
- low salaries;
- inadequate administrative systems (filing, registration of contracts, regulation of fees, etc);
- heavy caseloads;
- insufficient physical facilities; and
- corruption at all levels.

Problems related to the laws themselves emanate primarily from inconsistencies and contradictions between *'urf* and codified laws.

Access to the legal system is critical for the rule of law. Potential litigants in Yemen are discouraged from using the legal system. Many people are not sure whether they should seek redress from tribal or from state institutions. For

85. In Yemen's third largest city, Ta'izz, households receive public water once every 30-40 days (US State Department 1997, p4).
86. In 1990/91 a Ministry of Education survey found that 49 per cent of primary schools had no electricity, 47 per cent had no water and 44 per cent had no toilets (*Children and Women in Yemen: A Situation Analysis 1998*, Vol. III, p11).

---

11. SHAYKHLY IMMUNITY

Traditionally, some *mashayikh* (tribal leaders) were *hijrah* or *muhajjar*, 'set aside' or 'protected' from tribal conflict, a concept similar to the principle that protects settlements and markets (see page 23). This form of *shaykhly* 'immunity' contributes to lawlessness among this social group, evident in clashes with citizens and security forces, and in illegal seizures of property. Such behaviour may be further encouraged by external actors. An example of *mashayikh* operating outside the rule of law is the common practice of holding people in private jails while they await tribal judgment. These facilities are often well hidden and unsupervised, and many are believed to be inhumane. In April 2000, an incident of illegal and cruel incarceration received national attention. Two *shaykhs* from Dhamar imprisoned seven young men, accused of theft, without food or water in a poorly ventilated metal container for three days. Four of the men died, two became insane and one was critically injured. While *mashayikh* are not alone in considering themselves above the law, *shaykhly* extralegal behaviour is common and contributes to the perception that the rule of law applies only to the weak and vulnerable.

Based on Dresch (1995) and (1989) and *Yemen Times*, 24-30 April 2000

women, cultural norms inhibit entry to the legal system because the process is male dominated, although female lawyers are increasingly common and female judges preside over some southern courtrooms. The expense of pursuing a legal case favours wealthier litigants. For rural people, given the inadequate infrastructure of the courts, the distance and expense of staying in urban centres to pursue a case is prohibitive. Ignorance of legal rights is exacerbated by high levels of illiteracy (particularly among women). Judges and legal professionals are subjected to intimidation by powerful litigants and the state is frequently unable to enforce legal rulings. All this clearly inhibits confidence in the legal system and the judiciary and blocks access to the rule of law for those who need it most: the poor, rural and female.

Historically there has been frequent tension in Yemen between the state and the tribes. Until today, the state authority has been unable to penetrate many aspects of life in northern tribal areas. There are many reasons for this, both historical and contemporary, but the overriding fact is that the heavily armed tribes resist subjection to outside authority. Thus central government intervention in local matters can carry a high political and military cost. This tribal independence and power have been important in moderating abuses of authority by the state. However, since 1990 there has been an increase in violence in tribal areas – between individuals and tribes and against outsiders (tourists, oil workers, Yemenis travelling through), with the state unable to impose the rule of law. The violence includes carjacking, blood feuds, sabotaging of oil facilities, smuggling and bombings.[87] As a result of tribe-state tensions, government service delivery and channels for *qaba'il* to participate in democratic institutions have been limited. This has exacerbated the distrust of and disenchantment with state authority among the approximately 27 tribes of Yemen's highlands.

Another example of the government's inability to enforce the rule of law is kidnapping of foreigners and other Yemenis. Most such kidnappings are a mechanism to pressure the government to provide a service (such as a clinic or school), fulfil a previous promise of a service, or to seek redress for a perceived injustice (such as release of a fellow tribesman imprisoned for a tribally accepted action such as participating in a blood feud). While kidnapping is of recent origin, over the past decade a code of accepted rules and behaviour has developed for both the kidnappers and the government.[88] Between 1996 and July 2000 there were 40 incidents of foreigners being kidnapped, involving 149 hostages, 112 of them tourists.[89] Although nearly all hostages were safely released, the few tragedies and the frequency of kidnapping have badly damaged Yemen's economy and perceptions of security. Despite government efforts, tribal kidnappings have continued, although the number of incidents has decreased since 1997.[90]

A potential challenge to the rule of law in Yemen is the rise of militant Islamists. One spark for the increased activity of such groups has been the return of *mujahideen* from Afghanistan.[91] These Islamist movements are variously labelled as 'Afghan Arabs', Wahhabi, or *salafi*[92] (puritan). The more extreme elements operate outside the mainstream and choose to influence mosque politics, or combat 'impurity' in underground activities which have included vandalising pre-Islamic monuments and tombs of saints, as well as harassing those they perceive as not true Muslims. The most extreme elements have been involved in terrorist activities that included participation by

87. See US State Department (1999) p27 for examples of tribal violence.
88. Traditional hospitality is extended to the guests and the resolution of the incident is governed by time-honoured mechanisms of negotiation.
89. Security Incidents in Yemen 1990-94 and 1999 at: www.al-bab.com/yemen.
90. A number of factors may have contributed to this decline, including: a 1998 presidential decree imposing severe punishments for kidnapping, carjacking, and sabotage; establishing a special court to prosecute such crimes; numerous convictions of kidnappers; and the Saudi-Yemeni border agreement of 2000.
91. While waging a *jihad* (holy war) against the Soviet invasion these volunteers received military training, religious indoctrination and raising of their political consciousness. The Yemeni *mujahideen* were often recruited from poor rural families
92. A movement designed to purify other corrupted Muslims and eradicate Western and *kafir* (infidel) influence in order to create a pure Muslim state. It should be noted that few *salafiyeen* advocate violence, or are involved in politics. Nevertheless, their bearded chins, unwillingness to shake hands with women and extremely conservative attitudes distinguish them from other Yemenis.

non-Yemenis.[93] Although their numbers remain small, the weakness of the rule of law, the opportunities presented by democratisation, and the swelling ranks of the disenfranchised may contribute to an expanding militant Islamist influence in Yemen.[94]

Reform

With donor assistance, the government has undertaken a wide range of reforms intended to improve governance. These measures will attempt to:

- strengthen economic and financial management ability;
- improve tax and customs administration;
- improve budget management and monetary policy; and
- modernise the civil service and expand institutional capacity.

Following the economic reform process initiated in the mid-1990s with donor assistance the government began a judicial reform process and this has continued with a recent phase focusing on the Ministries of Justice and of Legal and Parliamentary Affairs.[95] In 1999 a number of security officials were convicted and punished for human rights abuses, but there were no further prosecutions in 2000. In September 2000 the first group of female police officers in the ROY graduated.[96] It is anticipated that they will reduce abuses by security forces against female prisoners and victims of violence against women. Civil service reform efforts have targeted selective ministries for reform, reducing the workforce (by retiring or laying off employees with more than one government position), increasing salaries, training, and upgrading systems and facilities.

3. Democratisation

The ROY was established on the principles of political pluralism, liberalisation of the economy, opening up of society, democratisation and decentralisation. Democratisation has progressed steadily over the past decade despite political, economic and social problems. Yemen is the only country on the Arabian Peninsula that enjoys universal suffrage. During the 1990s citizen participation in political parties increased, a relatively free press developed, and non-governmental organisations (NGOs) expanded significantly. The remaining challenges include:

93. Terrorist activities include the December 1998 kidnapping of 16 Western tourists in Mudiyah, various bomb attacks and the USS Cole explosion in October 2000 (which killed 17 and injured 39 American sailors).
94. See Carapico (2000) for more detailed analysis of neo-Islamist movements in Yemen at: www.merip.org/pins/pin35.html.
95. This phase of reform will: provide training in business and commercial law for judges; enhance the legal education curriculum; improve the capacity to draft legislation; review commercial laws for gaps and inconsistencies; increase budgets and judges salaries; and provide training for judicial staff.

96. When the government announced the recruitment of candidates to fill the 60 positions allotted for female officers, not only did a heated debate ensue in society about the appropriateness of this action, but also more than 2,000 young women from all parts of the country applied. The authorities subsequently increased the quota of female officers but were nevertheless forced to turn away hundreds of applicants.

- improving protection of human rights and freedom of expression;
- addressing citizen needs; and
- expanding decision-making structures to enable greater participation of women and marginalised groups.

Democratic institutions

Since unification Yemen has held two nation-wide constitutional referenda (1991 and 2001), two parliamentary elections (1993 and 1997), a presidential election (1999) and local council elections (2001). The Supreme Elections Committee (SEC) is the only independent permanent election body in the Arab world with broad responsibilities (that it has not always been able to meet).[97] Nevertheless, the consensus among local and international observers of the 1993 and 1997 parliamentary elections was that they were generally free and fair. Although the 1999 presidential election was less than competitive, the pattern of increasing female participation has continued (16 per cent in 1993, 28 per cent in 1997 and 38 per cent in 1999). The duties and responsibilities of the upper legislative chamber, established in the 2001 constitutional referendum, will be developed in the coming years. The local council elections in February 2001 were marked by violence and disorganisation, but have the potential to increase community participation and improve government services by decentralising many aspects of government. The electoral experiences and democratic institutions developed between 1990 and 2001 have influenced citizens' expectations and shaped political, economic and social developments. Democratic processes, although not without their flaws, are evident in parliamentary debates over legislation and policy that are televised and widely watched.

An essential component of democratisation is political pluralism. During the 1990s the number of political parties decreased, but those that remain have improved their internal management and become more responsive to the public. Since unification three political parties have led the field. The General People's Congress (GPC), established in 1982, was the YAR ruling party and has remained in power in the unified state. The Yemeni Socialist Party (YSP) was the junior partner in 1990-94, and since 1994 has been the leading opposition party. The conservative Islamic Yemeni Reform Gathering (referred to as Islah) was established in 1990 by Shaykh 'Abd Allah Ibn Husayn al-Ahmar, the powerful head of the Hashid Confederation (and Speaker of the Parliament since 1993).

Since unity there has been a fair degree of competition between the three major parties at the polls and in Parliament. Although the GPC has maintained its leadership, with a majority in both the 1993 and 1997 Parliaments, the YSP recovered some of its political influence in the later half of the 1990s. Throughout the decade Islah played a major role in state institutions and the political arena through the tremendous influence wielded by Shaykh al-Ahmar. There is also a degree of internal rivalry within each party. For example, the role of women in leadership has created controversy in all three major parties. After much debate and discussion even Islah, the most conservative, now has seven women (out of 130 members – 5.3 per cent) on its Supreme Council. As one party official stated, 'Because this divisive issue was resolved in a democratic manner, even those that still opposed women's involvement respected the changes in the party.'[98] In all parties the number of women in leadership positions is small, but the debate has clearly established a precedent for women's active participation.[99]

97. The SEC mandate includes: voter education and registration; equipping polling stations and training poll workers; establishing systems for counting votes; arranging for campaign media for parties and candidates; and coordinating election security, as well as local and international observers.
98. Personal interview with Mr Abdullah Muhsin al-Akwa, Islah Party Director of External Relations, May 2000.
99. The GPC has 52 women on its Permanent Committee (out of 501 —10.3 per cent), one woman (out of 20) on the party s General Committee and two female MPs elected in 1997. The YSP Central Committee has 28 female members (out of 301 — 9.3 per cent) and in the party s Fourth Annual Congress in August 2000, four women were elected to the Political Bureau.

Civil society

The term 'civil society' encompasses formal and informal voluntary associations organised around common interests. In the democratisation process, civil society can strengthen and enhance democratic institutions and structures. It can provide opportunities for citizens to gain skills and experience in articulating ideas, working with others and developing leadership skills. In Yemen, civil society includes labour organisations, farmer cooperatives, tribal confederations, mutual self-help and Islamic associations, all loosely described as non-governmental organisations (NGOs). The competition of ideas – in the media, academia and broader society – is an important aspect of a thriving civil society that has grown significantly since unification.

Community activism and civil society in Yemen did not begin with unification. There were two earlier periods when the political climate encouraged community activism. The first was in Aden under the British rule, from the 1950s to the 1960s, when the colonial administration authorised trades unions, proposed constitutions and held elections for a minority of seats on the Legislative Council. The second was in the YAR in the 1970s and early 1980s, when popularly elected LDAs flourished, affording participation and popular expression in communities around the country. The early years of unification (1990-94) saw a third period of civil society activity in Yemen: the government exerted limited control, and freedom of speech, the media and NGO activity expanded. The 1994 civil war signalled a tightening of government restrictions in many areas, including civil society.[100]

A survey in 1997 found approximately 1,215 NGOs registered in Yemen.[101] By 2000 the number had nearly doubled to between 2,000 and 2,500 organisations addressing a wide range of cultural, social, economic and political issues. Most NGOs are relatively young and have a limited membership base, although rural agricultural cooperatives and charitable organisations with larger memberships are becoming increasingly common.[102] Whether urban or rural, most NGOs face similar problems: lack of cooperative leadership skills; financial instability; administrative and management weaknesses; weak institutional capacity; and limited membership base. Moreover, the legal environment for NGOs is in transition. The first law passed in 2001, replacing YAR legislation dating from 1963, was the Associations and Foundations Law regulating procedures for establishing, operating and monitoring non-governmental associations. Although it clarified some legal and procedural issues, this law could also limit growth of the voluntary sector.

From 1990 to 1994 political discourse was relatively unfettered. In the early 1990s more than 50 newspapers and 60 periodicals were published regularly.[103] However, since the 1994 civil war, journalists, editors and publishers frequently report restrictions, harassment and arbitrary arrest.[104] Despite increasing government censorship, Yemen's press, with more than 60 non-government-sponsored publications, remains among the region's freest. The media frequently publish open criticism of the government, drawing attention to abuses and violations of human rights by the security forces. In private and public fora a lively debate continues regarding critical issues, with negligible government monitoring or interference. Many local and international NGOs operating in Yemen are dedicated to monitoring and protecting freedom of the press and the expression of ideas. In 2000 it was estimated that the country had 16,000 internet

100. This paragraph is based on the work of Sheila Carapico (1998).
101. *Children and Women in Yemen: A Situation Analysis 1998*, Vol 1, p14.
102. One type of rural community-based organisation that has become more common is the farmers association. In 1994 the government passed legislation encouraging such associations and by 1999 one farmer in 10 belonged to such associations. (World Bank 1999, p6)
103. Whitaker (2000a), p1.
104. US State Department (1999), p13.

users and 5,400 subscribers.[105] Internet service has few restrictions and the number of internet cafés and other fee-based access points is increasing. However, access remains prohibitively expensive for most Yemenis. Despite these challenges and constraints, Yemeni civil society holds great potential (in an environment which enables the relatively free exchange of ideas) and influences.

Marginalised groups

The term 'marginalised' refers to social groups that are denied full participation in society because of ethnicity, social status or 'undesirable' physical characteristics. In Yemen marginalised groups include *akhdam* (meaning 'servants'), *muwalideen* (Yemenis of mixed ancestry), refugees and people with disabilities. Individuals in these groups encounter discrimination from the government bureaucracy and in broader society. Many have limited tribal or traditional protection and have lower rates of literacy and education. For a variety of reasons the poor, the young and rural people are also, by default, disenfrachised. Unification and democratisation have raised their expectations, creating an awareness of their marginal status as well as frustration at unfulfilled promises. Materialistic advertising and conspicuous consumption by elites have helped create new perceptions of poverty and the poor in Yemen.

The origins of Yemen's *akhdam* are uncertain. The most common explanation is that they are the remnants of ancient Ethiopian invasions. Whatever their origin, they clearly were (and still are) the lowest traditional status group in Yemen, and many barriers remain to their full participation in society. Revolutions in both the former north and south officially abolished distinctions based on social class. Nevertheless, *akhdam* continue to perform 'unclean' tasks such as collecting garbage and sweeping the streets. Further stigma is attached to them because many *akhdam* children and women beg to make ends meet. It is currently estimated that there are 200,000 *akhdam*, primarily clustered in shantytowns in San'a', Hodeidah, Aden and Zabid.

Muwalideen, particularly of African and Indian ancestry, often encounter discrimination in society and in government bureaucracies. Although such discrimination is not sanctioned by law or official policy, negative attitudes towards those with darker skin and African or Asian features is common.

There is significant commercial, political and social contact between Yemen and the Horn of Africa. Although Yemen was one of the few Arab countries to accede to the 1951 Geneva Convention on the Status of Refugees and its 1967 Protocol, the legal status of refugees in Yemen does not conform with this international treaty.[106] Nevertheless, between 1990 and 2000 an estimated 500,000 Africans passed through Yemen.[107] While Yemen has usually welcomed those fleeing economic, political and natural disasters in Africa, the government has limited resources and donor assistance is minimal. High unemployment among Yemenis, and discrimination against those with darker skin, have contributed to local resentment. Both refugees and undocumented immigrants are commonly pressured for bribes by government officials and security personnel, and are often subjected to harassment by employers, landlords and businesses. Women refugees suffer from stereotypes that African women are morally loose, have limited employment potential (largely domestic help) and are vulnerable to abuse by employers (such as withholding of wages). These women often have special health needs owing to the high incidence of female

105. US State Department (2000), p12
106. UNDP (2001) p18.
107. *Refugees Daily*, 13 January 1999, at: www.unhcr.org

12. HIV/AIDS IN YEMEN

In 1987 a Yemeni student who had studied abroad was diagnosed as the first case of AIDS in Yemen. By August 2000 the number of documented cases of HIV/AIDS in the country had reached 1,500. Issues of concern regarding HIV/AIDS in Yemen are:

- The official statistics are clearly inaccurate. Yemen's inadequate health care system and the lack of equipment to test HIV/AIDS outside major urban centres guarantees that many cases are undiagnosed.
- Given the medical treatment available in Yemen, those who develop AIDS are unlikely to receive adequate care. And those testing HIV positive are likely to encounter discrimination and punishment rather than treatment. Africans testing positive are likely to be deported and it is not uncommon that HIV positive Yemenis will be rejected by their families and society.
- Safe sex education presents challenges as sex education is not part of the pre-collegiate curriculum. Also, taboos against discussing sexual matters in mixed gender settings, even between spouses, have already posed a challenge in family planning. Practices such as polygamy and legal requirements that a wife provide sexual access to her husband increase women's vulnerability to the spread of HIV/AIDS.
- Actions intended to prevent the spread of HIV could reinforce discrimination, strengthen conservative agendas or further threaten marginalised populations. At the time of writing, all foreign workers in Yemen must undergo HIV tests to obtain work or residence visas. Affluent expatriates use private laboratories for such tests because the government facilities, although inexpensive, can be unclean and use unsafe testing practices. Expatriates with fewer resources, including refugees and immigrants, are at risk of HIV infection from the testing because of their economic status.
- Other important issues for HIV/AIDS in Yemen include: the practice of female genital mutilation as a potential avenue for infection; the high incidence of HIV/AIDS among individuals with sexually transmitted diseases; the lack of resources to address the issue; and the absence of a clear and well-funded government programme.

To date donors and NGOs have supported or implemented very few education programmes. Coordination between government agencies, donors, and potential partners to address the spread of HIV/AIDS has generally been lacking. However, it is anticipated that the Second National Five-Year Plan currently being drafted will address the issue.

Based on information from *Yemen Times* 21-27 August 2000 and UN (2001) p 6.

genital mutilation (FGM) and HIV/AIDS among them (see box 13). However, many local and international NGOs are helping the ROY government and the UN High Commissioner on Refugees (UNHCR) to address the needs of refugees. Since July 1994 CIIR/ICD has been providing health care for refugees under the auspices of UNHCR in San'a'.

Another particularly vulnerable group are women with disabilities. Estimates place the number of people with disabilities at 115,000, 47 per cent of them female and 53 per cent male.[108] Men with disabilities face discrimination related to their condition: their ability to marry, work and participate in society depends on the nature and severity of their disability. This is not the case for women with disabilities, who are less likely to marry and to receive health care and education. The illiteracy rate for women with disabilities is estimated at 95 per cent.

Another increasingly marginalised sector of the population is the poor. In 1997, an unofficial estimate was that 30 per cent of the Yemen's population lived below the poverty line. Unemployment, estimated at 40 per cent, has

108. National Women's Committee (1999) p18.

greatly increased their numbers.[109] As a group, they lack organisation to participate in politics, and thus their needs are often ignored by decision-making structures. Among the poor are growing numbers of young men. With more than 50 per cent of the population under the age of 15, many young men have few resources and limited opportunities for work, whether inside or outside the country, and the infrastructure is ill-equipped to provide them with education or skills.

The discourse on democratisation poses significant questions for citizens, elected officials, the government and donors. Failure to meet the basic needs of citizens for food and shelter could jeopardise the democratic experiment. Citizens' frustration that the 1990s have not yielded the benefits they expected and that were promised to them may lead to apathy, alienation and possibly violence.

4. Gender and development[110]

The terms sex and gender distinguish biologically distinct attributes (childbearing and breastfeeding; impregnation) from socially constructed roles, responsibilities and relations of men and women. Gender roles and relations change over time and vary according to social, educational and cultural factors. In Yemen, the concept of gender, often misunderstood, is highly controversial. At the core of the debate are perspectives on appropriate relations between men and women and how these building blocks relate to visions of society. Men and women in the media, on campuses, in the corridors of government and in the home are struggling with these issues.

Gender relations in Yemen are shaped by diverse religious, cultural, social and political traditions. Sources of this diversity include the differing legal, political and economic environments in the former YAR and PDRY. Among Yemen's geographic regions, different gender roles and relations are found on the

109. US State Department (1999) p2.

110. This section draws heavily on writing and research on gender and development in Yemen conducted by the author for Oxfam UK in 2000, to be published in 2002.

---

13. AN ADENI VOICE: NAWAL ANWAR KHAN

'My father's great-grandfather arrived in Aden in 1839 from India as a British soldier. My father was the first in his family to marry a Yemeni. My mother's father was from Bait al-Faqih (on the Tihamah) and my grandmother was Moroccan. During the 1970s and 1980s Aden was a place where strong women were supported in their endeavours. Growing up, women excelled in many aspects of life. For example, I participated from a young age in the active network of sports and youth clubs that were found throughout the city of Aden. Athletic abilities in swimming and running were encouraged and as a result I travelled widely throughout the world competing at international sports events. There were 15 women competing on the national sports team. During that era, if a student excelled, they were given opportunities to study. I went to Tashkent, Uzbekistan, and received my MA in journalism. Now, for me in Aden, there are two sets of prejudices that I face daily – being a half-caste and a strong woman. For some women it has been easier to adjust dress, attitude and behaviour, but I was raised differently. I am not ready to lose my freedom.'

Based on a personal interview.

Tihamah, in the Wadi Hadhramaut and Hujariyyah, among urban dwellers in San'a' and Aden, on island communities and in tribal areas in the east and the northern highlands. Degrees of sex segregation, mobility and educational options vary widely for women in Yemen. They depend not only on their region of origin, but also on their social and economic status. There are also important differences between rural and urban women with regard to educational opportunities, access to health care, the gender division of labour, the number of children they have, and gender relations.

Tribal traditions and status inequalities based on occupation and ancestry provide an essential background to gender inequalities that are woven into the texture of urban and rural life. One source, and justification, for status and gender inequalities is that greater responsibilities mean higher status and therefore, more rights and privileges. Women are considered 'weak' (*du'afa*) and therefore 'protected.' While women bear considerable productive and reproductive responsibilities, these roles are accorded lower status than those of men (protecting, defending, external relations, farming the land, and so on). Status inequalities are also found within families and among the tribes. In the domestic realm the patriarch is the ultimate decision-maker, ruling alongside his wife, who controls most essential domestic decisions. Economic decisions and external relations are largely the responsibility of men. Women have primary responsibility in domestic affairs, as well as for decisions related to livestock, processing of dairy and food items and agricultural tasks.

The legal context

Key gender issues in the legal sphere include legal professionals, access to courts, legal literacy, and discrepancies in rights and in the application and enforcement of laws. Gender inequities in inheritance laws disadvantage women in several ways. With few exceptions, a woman's share of a male's estate is half that of the equivalent male relative.[111] Yemen's penal codes emphasise women's limited rights as legal and social persons subordinate to the authority of male family members. In addition to statutory gender inequities, police behaviour and judicial interpretation often punish female victims rather than male criminals.

The Personal Status Law of 1992 is based primarily on the 1979 YAR Family Law, with a few minor changes. It contravenes the Convention on the Elimination of all forms of Discrimination Against Women (CEDAW) – to which Yemen is nominally bound by the PDRY ratification in 1984 – in the following ways:

- silence of the bride is interpreted as consent in marriage;
- the wife is required to provide sexual access to her husband (disallowing rape within marriage);
- the wife requires the permission of her husband to leave the house except to attend to the needs of her parents;
- polygamy is legal, although the first wife must be informed if her husband is marrying another;
- women enter the marital contract through male relatives or a judge;
- unequal grounds for divorce are required from men and women;[112]
- in divorce the law grants the mother custody until her children are of age (nine for male children and 12 for female) on condition of her maturity, sanity, faithfulness, moral and physical ability or if she remarries.[113]

111. Two noted exceptions are that of a uterine sister inheriting equally with her brother and a mother and father inheriting equally from their deceased child (Glander, 1999, p78).

112. Women have the legal right to sue for divorce, but unlike men they must provide justification, for example : a defect in the marriage contract or the person; *darar* (damage) as a result of prolonged absence, non-payment of maintenance, alcohol or drug abuse; and *karahiya* (deep hatred). Other legally admissible justifications for divorce include adultery, impotence, disease (for example, leprosy), or marriage to a second wife without permission. Men have the prerogative of unilateral divorce (Würth 1995, p324).

113. For full text of the CEDAW (1979) and the Beijing Platform (1995) see: www.feminist.org/research/cedaw/main.html.

A woman who initiates divorce must return the *mahr* (variously translated as dowry, bridal payment or bride-wealth – a payment made from the groom to the bride at the time of the marriage contract). This law discourages women from seeking divorce.

Discrepancies between legal rights and actual practices are significant. For example, although the legal minimum age of marriage is 15 for males and females, violations of this law are common. The median age of marriage for urban women is 17.6 years and for rural women 15.9 years. A study in 1992 found that 9 per cent of girls between the ages of 15 and 19 at the time of the survey had been married by their 15th birthday.[114] A further example of a discrepancy between law and practice takes place when a woman applies for a Yemeni passport. The 'Passport Law' does not have gender requirements for issuing a passport, but in practice a woman seeking a passport must have a male sponsor.

Rural life

Women face additional challenges and have different needs from those of their fathers, brothers, husbands and sons. For example, the burden of rural women's productive roles, high fertility levels, and cultural and economic factors constrain their mobility, encourage illiteracy (65 per cent nationally for women, compared with 32 per cent for men) and damage their health. Research from the late 1980s estimated that female farmers did more than 70 per cent of the agricultural work in the YAR.[115] The exact productive roles of women vary regionally, seasonally and with the crop, and the presence or absence of male labour, as well as age, economic and social status. However, in much of Yemen female farmers perform the most labour-intensive tasks, relying on manual labour or simple tools. Yemeni women farmers usually cultivate rain-fed land and produce basic food

114. *Children and Women in Yemen: A Situation Analysis 1998*, Vol I, p125.
115. Buringa (1988) p12.

---

14. A BIOGRAPHY OF ACTIVISM: FATIMAH HURAYBI HASSAN

Fatimah Huraybi Hassan was educated in Aden and the United States, with a Bachelor of Science degree in Agriculture from Michigan State University (1975) and a Bachelor of Arts in Sociology and Women's Studies from Wayne State University (1985). She has worked in the Ministry of Agriculture and Irrigation since 1975 and at the time of writing is the head of the training department. In 1994 she began working part-time for Yemeni Television and Radio as an English-language news announcer. In the local council elections in February 2001 she was elected to represent her San'a' neighbourhood. Based on her expertise in rural agriculture, Fatimah feels that mobility is one of the primary challenges in rural women's lives, affecting their own health and that of their children, as well as their economic status. In Yemen there are very few places where women can market the products of their labour. Other major challenges facing women in general, and female farmers specifically, are land ownership and the lack of credit for investment in income-generating projects. In the Wadi Hadhramaut, Fatimah met women in Ghayl ba-Wazir who had researched the possibility of establishing a bakery for *ruti* (a type of bread) and other baked goods, but who lacked the capital to put their ideas into practice. Female farmers and rural women are also harmed by: increasingly conservative attitudes; lack of female agricultural extension agents; poor health and a lack of affordable services; and growing levels of rural poverty, to which women are particularly vulnerable.

Based on personal interview.

crops for family consumption. Throughout Yemen female farmers are generally responsible for animals. In addition to women's reproductive (cooking, housework and childcare) and agricultural tasks they are usually responsible for grinding grain by hand, hauling water, collecting fuel and fodder, making dung cakes, applying organic fertiliser, drying grains, and storing, preserving and processing food.[116]

The public arena

Yemeni women were the first, and remain the only, females on the Arabian Peninsula to gain the right to vote. While women in Kuwait, the Kingdom of Saudi Arabia and other Gulf states are struggling for this essential right, women in Yemen have been able to vote for decades. Also unique is their opportunity to participate in multi-party politics. In the last decade women increased their influence in the three major political parties. The Islah party, with a conservative religious platform, has attracted the largest number of female voters. The Yemeni government has also attempted to integrate more women into the state bureaucracy. Since 1995 there have been some ground-breaking developments for women:

- in the 2000 Olympics Hana 'Ali Saleh, a 32 year-old Adeni mother of two, competed in the 200-metre sprint, becoming the first ROY female athlete to participate in the Olympics;
- in February 2001 Captain Roza 'Abdul al-Khaliq was the first Yemeni woman to pilot an official plane;
- in 2000 Her Excellency Amat al-Aleem Assooswa was appointed ROY ambassador to the Netherlands; and
- in March 2001 a woman, Dr Wahiba Far'a', was appointed Minister of Human Rights.

These may seem small steps, but they do indicate government support for women's equal participation in public life, despite the culturally conservative context.[117]

Education and health

Female literacy rates are extremely low: 35 per cent in 1998 compared to a male rate of 69 per cent. Real government spending on education decreased by 28 per cent between 1990-93 and 1994-96.[118] Yemen's population explosion has increased the pressure on school buildings and staff and falling government education budgets have only exacerbated this. Female teachers are relatively few and are clustered in urban areas, and there is a general lack of schools, of sex-segregated schools in particular. Social attitudes favour male education over female. Although primary education is free and compulsory, parental attitudes are important in determining whether or not children attend. A study of attitudes to girls' education in 1995 found that most of those surveyed felt that it was less important to educate girls than boys.[119] A 1997 UNICEF study found that 69 per cent of parents agreed in principle that girls should be educated, although support for female education was much higher in urban than in rural areas – 91 per cent compared with 41 per cent.[120]

Fewer girls than boys enrol in school, and a higher proportion drop out. Early marriages often prevent girls from completing their studies. Also, the cost

116. Much of this paragraph is based on information from Mundy (1995).
117. The former PDRY fielded numerous female athletes (primarily from Aden) in national, regional and international sports events, but Ms Saleh was the first woman to represent the ROY in the Olympics.
118. *Children and Women in Yemen: A Situation Analysis 1998*, Vol. I, p. 77.
119. *Ibid*, p15.
120. *Ibid*, p16.

of travel to school, fees, textbooks, stationery and uniforms reinforces negative attitudes toward female education. For rural families, the loss of labour when girls attend school is significant. Other factors which discourage girls' education include the distance to school, the lack of female teachers, mixed gender classrooms and inadequate facilities (only 49 per cent of primary schools have electricity; 47 per cent have no water and 44 per cent have no toilets).[121]

Currently, health care in Yemen is inadequate. Government spending on health is decreasing not only as a proportion of the budget (in 1990 it was 4.2 per cent and in 1997 it was 3.1 per cent) but also in terms of *per capita* spending (from US$8.00 in the early 1990s to US$3.60 in 1997). Yemen has a very high infant and child mortality rate – 83 and 110 respectively out of 1,000 live births, compared to the Middle East regional average which is 46 and 60 out of 1,000. Key gender issues that contribute to this situation are:

- low maternal literacy;
- high fertility rates;
- maternal age and general health;
- access to and quality of maternal health care services; and
- the heavy workload of rural mothers.

Maternal health issues begin with Yemen's extraordinarily high fertility rates. Women aged 15-49 years had a total fertility rate of 6.5 live children, with urban women averaging 6.25 children and rural women, on average, giving birth to eight. The rate of maternal mortality is high – estimated at between 1,000 and 1,400 per 100,000 births. The main reasons for this include poor nutrition (35 per cent of Yemeni women are anaemic), distance from health facilities, the expense of seeking health care, maldistribution and lack of trained medical

121. *Ibid*, p31.

DINNY HAWES/CIIR-ICD

Yemeni women are unique among women on the Arabian Peninsula in having the right to vote.

personnel to attend births (in 1997 only 22 per cent of births were attended by trained personnel) and limited emergency obstetric services for rural populations.

Women's health is also affected by female circumcision. Female circumcision is the form of female genital mutilation (FGM) which cuts the prepuce or hood of the clitoris.[122] The most common estimate of its incidence in Yemen is between 10 and 20 per cent of all women, with a slightly higher rate among older women. The practice is not sanctioned in Islam, although it is found in many Muslim countries, particularly in Africa. In Yemen it is most common along the coast, where African culture has had greatest impact, and among social groups such as the *akhdam*. However, among African refugees and immigrants the more extreme forms of FGM – excision and infibulation – are practised.[123] FGM causes physical and psychological damage, particularly when conducted in unhygienic conditions using traditional tools. The 1997 Demographic Survey found that 97 per cent of female circumcisions were performed at home by older women or traditional birth attendants.[124] On 10 January 2001, the Minister of Health publicised a ministerial resolution banning female circumcision in hospitals in Yemen. Given that most FGM procedures are conducted outside the health care system, this is unlikely to have much impact.

Inequalities of gender and status are intertwined in the practices of female seclusion and veiling (covering the face). The practice of sequestering women – protecting them from work, from public view, violence and interactions with strangers – was traditionally found only among the religious elite and wealthier families. Veiling gained popularity in urban areas after its introduction during the Ottoman occupations. By the 20th century, in most urban areas throughout Yemen women in all status groups, except the lowest, veiled themselves and attempted to practice female seclusion and sex segregation. Despite the urban trend of veiling, women in rural Yemen do not generally cover their faces and tend to wear brightly coloured clothing according to regional styles. One elderly woman from the south summarised a common rural attitude: 'The veil is for the town woman who sits all day in her house. It is not for we [sic] women who work.'[125] Rural women's productive and reproductive roles require physical mobility and movement away from home to farm and bring water, fodder and fuel. While these activities are often done by groups of women, the need for mobility brings them into regular contact with men from their community, although in social settings men and women rarely mingle. When paved roads arrive in rural communities, there is a noticeable increase in women covering their faces. However, when women who normally go unveiled leave their rural community, they cover their faces and wear the *sharshif* (a three-tiered outfit consisting of a skirt, waist-length cape and head veil).

122. Minority Rights Group (1985) p3.
123. Excision (the cutting of the clitoris and all or part of the labia minora) or infibulation (the cutting of the clitoris, labia minora and at least the anterior two-thirds and often the whole of the medial part of the labia majora) are two extreme forms of this practice. Infibulation is commonly practised in Somalia, Djibouti and the Sudan, southern Egypt, the Red Sea coast of Ethiopia and northern Kenya, all areas with long-standing ties to Yemen (*ibid*).
124. National Women's Committee (1999) p63.
125. Molyneux (1982) p15.

Conclusion

It is widely recognised in international development circles and by the Yemeni government that the participation of women, who are more than half of the population, is essential to meet the development challenges of the 21st century. Urban Yemeni women, and those with more formal education and greater affluence, are increasingly active in politics, civil society and the labour force. However, the productive and reproductive roles of women in rural areas continue to hinder their active participation in other aspects of community life. Cultural

15. COMPARING THE LIVES OR URBAN AND RURAL WOMEN

URBAN	RURAL
In 1994, 24 per cent of Yemen's population lived in urban areas	76 per cent of Yemenis live in communities with fewer than 500 residents
In urban areas and rural communities with high remittance levels, families are increasingly living in nuclear households, rather than in extended families	In villages, particularly where remittances were minimal, families still live predominantly in multi-generation households
The urban female literacy rate is 54 per cent	Female literacy in rural communities is 16 per cent
91 per cent of urban fathers favour girls' education	41 per cent of rural fathers agree in principle to girls' education
77.7 per cent of urban girls aged 6-15 are enrolled in school	24.2 per cent of rural girls aged 6-15 are enrolled in school
At the national level, by grade eight, only 19 per cent of the female student population who were once enrolled remain at school	In Al-Jawf, a remote area in the northeast, by grade eight only 10 per cent of girls once enrolled are still at school
In 1996, urban women had an average of 6.25 children	In 1996, rural women had an average of 7.95 children
39 per cent of urban women received no prenatal care before delivering their baby	73 per cent of rural women received no prenatal care before delivering their baby
61 per cent of urban women give birth attended by a trained birth attendant	37 per cent of rural women use the services of a trained birth attendant
In 1997, 36 per cent of urban women used contraception	In 1997, 16 per cent of rural women used contraception
94 per cent of urban households have access to safe drinking water	Less than half of rural households (49 per cent) have access to safe drinking water
In 1994, 91 per cent of urban households had access to adequate sanitation	In 1994, only 20 per cent of rural households had adequate sanitation
The median age for urban women to marry is 17.6 years	The median age for rural women to marry is 15.9 years
In 1996, the World Bank estimated that 19 per cent of Yemen's population were living below the poverty line; of that total 19 per cent lived in urban areas	The 1996 World Bank poverty study estimated that the majority of Yemen's poor, and those living in absolute poverty, live in rural areas

Source: ROY et al, Children and Women in Yemen: A Situation Analysis 1998.

traditions limit women's access to health care, education and family planning services. Finally, the economic challenges that Yemen faced in the last decade were disproportionately harmful to women. The recent *Interim Poverty Reduction Strategy Paper* noted that 'a female-headed households implies a higher risk of being poor by about 20%'.[126] Women are economically, socially and politically vulnerable, often with limited skills and support to improve their situation. For democratisation and development to continue to improve the lives of all Yemenis, women's participation in public life must increase.

126. Republic of Yemen (2000) p2.

5. Challenges for donors

Both the YAR and the PDRY received assistance for military, economic and human development from foreign governments (bilateral aid), inter-governmental organisations (multilateral aid) and international NGOs. In 1987 Official Development Assistance (ODA) to the YAR and the PDRY amounted to 8.1 per cent and 8.2 per cent of GNP, respectively.[127] The ROY government has continued this pattern of dependence on foreign donors, although the identity of donors and their priorities have changed over time. Table 5 summarises sources of

Table 5. Overview of major development assistance for 2000

Source of Aid	US Dollars	Per cent
Multilateral	**162,852,000**	**54.7**
World Bank	80,425,000	27.0
UN System	42,275,000	14.2
Arab Fund	22,009,000	7.4
EU	18,143,000	6.1
Bilateral	**133,520,000**	**44.8**
US	35,345,000	11.9
Germany	33,569,000	11.3
The Netherlands	28,627,000	9.6
Japan	27,400,000	9.2
All Others (Italy, France, UK)	8,579,000	2.8
International NGOs	**1,627,000**	**0.5**
(CARE, Oxfam, Radda Barnen)		
Total	**297,999,000**	**100**

Source: *2000 Annual Report of the United Nations Resident Coordinator: Republic of Yemen*

aid for 2000.

Since 1973 the World Bank and the IMF have consistently supported economic and human development in Yemen, providing more than US$1.7 billion to 118 projects. The World Bank increased its assistance dramatically in the mid-1990s to support the economic and government reform process. The various UN agencies have also been important multilateral donors for decades. After unification, UN assistance steadily increased, and by 1998 accounted for 10 per cent of ODA.[128] Other significant multilateral donors are the European Union and numerous Arab and Islamic organisations such as the Arab Fund for Economic and Social Development, the Islamic Development Bank, OPEC and the Arab Monetary Fund.

Bilateral assistance programmes in the 1990s have included a varying group of Asian (China, India, Indonesia, Japan and Korea), Islamic (Pakistan, Turkey), European and North American (Canada and the United States) governments. Also, many Arab countries have provided development aid to Yemen including Egypt, Jordan, Kuwait, Oman, Qatar, Saudi Arabia, Iraq and the United Arab Emirates. In 1999 the major bilateral donors to Yemen were Japan, the Netherlands, Germany, the United States, Italy, France and the United Kingdom.

127. Carapico (1998) p40.
128. UNDP (2001) p37.

Yemen including Irish Concern, Save the Children (US), Catholic Relief Services and others. However, today only a few maintain offices in the country.[129] Radda Barnen, International Cooperation for Development (ICD) and Oxfam UK have had the longest presence in Yemen.

Levels of aid plummetted after the Gulf War and in 1994 ODA amounted to only 3.4 per cent of GNP. However, after the United States, Saudi Arabia and Kuwait reduced their aid, other donors – including the Netherlands, Japan and Germany – increased their contributions. The IMF and the World Bank also increased their aid in support of the economic reform programme. By 1996 ODA had risen to 8.2 per cent of GNP, over 48 per cent of it funding economic management and only six per cent supporting health and human resource development.[130] Despite this, in 1998, according to the UNDP *Human Development Report 2000*, out of 34 countries in the category of Low Human Development, Yemen ranked 26th in terms of annual *per capita* aid, receiving US$18.8 for each Yemeni.

Yemen receives low levels of external aid partly because of its peripheral importance to geo-politics, as well as ignorance of its poverty in what is perceived as an oil-rich region. Donors also face challenges in project implementation. Lack of efficiency, accountability and transparency make it difficult to achieve programme objectives. The weakness of the rule of law creates an atmosphere often perceived as threatening to both Yemenis and expatriates. Effective assistance is complicated by:

- a lack of local skills and expertise;
- a limited range of community-based organisations or local partners to work with;
- unforeseen events such as war, natural disasters or terrorist activity; and
- difficulties in contacting and securing official approval for working with marginalised groups or communities.

129. These include: Adventist Development Relief Agency, AMIDEAST, Handicap International, International Foundation for Election Systems, National Democratic Institute, International Committee of the Red Cross, Marie Stopes International, Movi Mundo, Médecins Sans Frontières, Triangle, Friedrich Ebert Stiftung and CARE Australia.

130. *Children and Women in Yemen: A Situation Analysis 1998*, Vol 1, p15.

---

16. INTERNATIONAL COOPERATION FOR DEVELOPMENT (ICD)

ICD has been working with local partners to support development projects in Yemen since 1973. One of the first international NGOs to arrive in Yemen, ICD's co-operation has focussed on training and building the capacity of local partners through the placement of skilled development professionals particularly aiming to improve mother and child health. Significant health improvements have been gained for women and children both in access to health care and in its quality through systematic training of female primary health care workers (*murshidat*) and community midwives. In line with Yemen's changing national context and a new range of development challenges in the 21st century, ICD Yemen intends to support new initiatives within the Ministry of Public Health to introduce a decentralised, community managed system of health care delivery. In addition, ICD's skills sharing work will expand to support the range of capacity needs of civil society organisations including those with an interest in human rights, HIV/AIDS and support to women's groups.

The documentary film *Murshidat, Midwives and Nurses: Muslim Women Transforming Health Care and Social Relations in Yemen* shows some of the women trained in ICD's health project in Abs (see Recent Films on Yemen on page **) For further information on ICD/CIIR, see www.ciir.org

marginalised groups or communities.

At the same time, unequal power relations between funders and beneficiaries and contribute to complex dynamics and resentment of what are perceived as Western agendas being imposed on Yemen.[131]

Some development challenges affect larger bilateral and multilateral donor agencies in particular, limiting the positive impact of development assistance and sometimes producing unwanted results. For example:

- Donors do not always encourage collaboration and local input when selecting and planning projects. Projects may be identified on the basis of inadequate or faulty information, or of theoretical principles that do not necessarily apply in Yemen. International development specialists arrive in the country for identification and planning missions that are short on time and long on expectations; and they may be forced to use minimally qualified translators or local informants.
- Lack of coordination, cooperation and communication among donors can lead to duplication of efforts, confusion and repetition of mistakes. The Yemeni authorities do not always discourage this tendency, perhaps because of their own disorganisation or lack of communication and coordination.
- Large donor agencies are often bureaucratic and inflexible. Field offices and local missions struggle to have funds allocated to specific projects. Once funding is secured the donor's own bureaucratic procedures make it difficult to respond to changes on the ground or unforeseen expenses.
- Finally, donor agendas, decision-making and programme implementation procedures often lack transparency, accountability and efficiency. This example is not lost on Yemenis, who observe the gap between behaviour and rhetoric.

A critical issue for both donors and the government is to balance the need for basic services against the equally urgent requirement for structural reform to enable efficient service delivery. This realisation led such organisations as the World Bank, the IMF and UN agencies to step up support for capacity-building and institutional reform. The resources invested in institutional and economic reform have enabled Yemen to meet many of the conditions of its structural adjustment programme and to reduce its external debt. Nevertheless, by almost all measures real poverty has increased. The government has attempted to establish poverty alleviation programmes as a social safety net, but with little impact so far.

The ROY is currently preparing to join the World Trade Organisation. It is assumed that this move will improve relations with western governments and donors, and bring Yemen further into the global economy. However, serious concerns remain over the impact of globalisation on economies such as that of Yemen, as well as on people worldwide. It is unlikely that this move will improve Yemen's food security or decrease dependence on imported goods. Clearly, the ROY has learned that failure to cooperate with major donors has severe political and economic consequences.

131. For a thoughtful consideration of ethical and practical issues in implementing gender and development projects in Yemen see Gascoigne (1991).

V CONCLUSION

Table 6. Comparison of basic indicators: YAR, PDRY and ROY

Indicator	YAR	PDRY	ROY
Population (millions)	5.5 (1976)	1.5 (1972)	18.7 (1999)
Population growth rate	2.3% (1960)		3.7 (2000)
Life expectancy male/female	37/39 yrs (1970-75)	41/42 yrs (1970-75)	59.8 yrs (1999)
Adult literacy total/female	9%/1% (1970)	31%/9% (1970)	52%/36% (1998)
Population per doctor	56,150 (1965)	12,870 (1965)	4,700 (1999)
Population of capital city (thousands)	San a 120 (1973)	Aden 264 (1977)	San a 1,280 Aden 450 (1998)
Infant mortality	214/1,000 (1960)		80/1,000 (1998)
Child mortality (under five)	378/1,000 (1960)		122/1,000 (1992)
GNP per capita	US$390 (1976/7)	US$470 (1976)	US$275 (1999)
Enrolment of eligible students aged 6-15 years in basic education total/female	9%/1% (1965)	23%/10% (1965)	63%/40% (1997)
Asphalted roads	596 km (1972)	365 km (1973)	5,955 km

Sources: World Bank publications (1979) *YAR: Development of a Traditional Economy* and (1979) *PDRY: A Review of Economic and Social Development*; for health statistics for YAR and PDRY, Kemps and Staugard (1992) *Quality of Maternal and Neo-natal Health Services in Yemen*; ROY statistics, United Nations (2001) *Yemen Common Country Assessment and the Central Statistical Organization Statistical Yearbook 1998*.

Since the revolutions in the 1960s Yemen has made significant progress in terms of human development. Over the past four decades, improvements in infrastructure, literacy, life expectancy and infant, child and maternal mortality have been dramatic (see Table 6). Unfortunately, the crises and reform efforts of the 1990s have slowed many development activities.

In highlighting the development challenges facing Yemen, this report has focused on the issues that have slowed the pace of development. The list is long and may seem overwhelming, but there are also reasons for optimism about Yemen's future.

- Indigenous traditions provide opportunities to strengthen the democratisation process, improve citizen participation in governance and address environmental concerns.
- The ROY government has demonstrated its commitment to democratisation and, despite some citizen disappointment in the results, overwhelming popular support for the process remains.
- The decentralisation process initiated in February 2001 with the election of governorate and district councils has the potential to broaden citizens' participation in government and provide channels to involve marginalised social groups.
- Government support for female leadership and increasing female participation in public life is a sign of an increasingly responsive government.

- Although some aspects of civil society are more closely controlled by the government than in the early 1990s, the sector as a whole has been transformed by the decade of crisis and reform. Many local NGOs have matured in their capacity to engender social change.
- The development of the Port of Aden, anticipated revenues from natural gas, and other initiatives will strengthen the economy, although it will remain sensitive to external events.
- Improved relations with Oman, Eritrea and Saudi Arabia have paved the way for reduction of military spending, control of smuggling and regional economic cooperation.
- The reform of governance has the potential to increase accountability, transparency, capacity and efficiency and to address system-wide weaknesses.
- Economic reform has improved many economic indicators and, in combination with poverty alleviation programmes, may improve the economic status of citizens.

Donor cooperation has been critical for Yemen's development since the 1970s. Clearly, it will remain so in the 21st century. Government and donors must coordinate to combine their efforts and the knowledge gained from both successes and failures. The lessons learned from small-scale sustainable development projects, such as those implemented by ICD, provide critical input to policy and to project implementation. Whether in service delivery or in systemic reform, sustainable initiatives require adequate research and analysis, and collaboration between donors, the government and local project partners. The final component in community-based development is to establish partnerships with beneficiaries that build local leadership, vision and community support.

Travelling mountain roads, near Hajjarah.

ADAM BRADBURY/CIIR/ICD

PART 3 RESOURCES

Acronyms

CBO	Community-based organisation
EU	European Union
GDP	Gross domestic product
GNP	Gross national product
GPC	General People's Congress, a political party
ICD	International Cooperation for Development, a programme of CIIR
ICRC	International Committee of the Red Cross
IMF	International Monetary Fund
LCCDs	Local Councils for Cooperative Development
LDA	Local Development Association
NGO	Non-governmental organisation
NLF	National Liberation Front
OPEC	Organisation of Petroleum Exporting Countries.
ODA	Official development assistance
PDRY	People's Democratic Republic of Yemen
PRC	People's Republic of China
ROY	Republic of Yemen
SEC	Supreme Elections Committee
UNDP	United Nations Development Programme
UNFPA	United Nations Family Planning Association
UNICEF	United Nations International Children's Fund
UNHCR	United Nations High Commissioner for Refugees
USAID	United States Agency for International Development
YAR	Yemen Arab Republic, commonly referred to as North Yemen
YR	Yemeni rials
YSP	Yemeni Socialist Party

Glossary

akhdam (singular *khadim*) – 'servants'. A social group of uncertain origin (a common explanation is that they are the remnants of an unsuccessful Ethiopian invasion) who clearly occupy the lowest position in the traditional Yemeni social hierarchy. Although the social status of *akhdam* improved after the revolutions of the 1960s in north and south, many continue to work in what are considered to be 'dirty' jobs, such as sweeping the streets and collecting garbage.

hijar (singular *hijrah*) – sacred or protected. This status applies to numerous urban enclaves in Yemen, variously called *hijrah, haram* and *hawtah*, including San'a', Sa'dah, 'Amran, Khamir, Kawkaban, Shibam, Tarim and Manakha. It also applies to some tribal *mashayikh*.

Imam – the religious title that, in Yemeni history, refers to the theocratic Zaydi ruler chosen from among the *sadah* (descendents of the Prophet Mohammed) as the spiritual, temporal and military leader of the community. The Imamate was the institution of Zaydi rule over various parts of Yemen for nearly 1,000 years until the 1962 revolution. (See Zaydi Islam below.)

mashayikh (singular *shaykh*, literally meaning 'old man') – traditional tribal leaders of well-known ancestry. *Mashayikh* are often large landholders and their position in the tribe is based on their knowledge of tribal law and experience in arbitrating disputes. *Mashayikh* sometimes inherit their title, but are often elected to the position.

qabili (plural *qaba'il*) – tribesman. Traditionally the *qaba'il* combined the roles of farmer and warrior and embodied the values of autonomy and cooperation with members of one's tribe. Contemporary tribes that continue this system of values are largely confined to the Hashid and Bakil Confederations (see political actors, page 79).

qat – a shiny-leaved shrub cultivated extensively in Yemen. Its leaves are chewed on a daily basis by most men and increasing numbers of women, producing a mild stimulating and euphoric sensation. *Qat* afternoon gatherings are woven into cultural, professional and political traditions in Yemen. It is held that *qat* was first widely used in Yemen in the 14th or 15th century.

shari'ah – Islamic or canonical law which is based on four official sources: the *Qur'an*; the *Sunna* of the Prophet Mohammed – the normative model behaviour of the Prophet evidenced in what he did, and those actions that he permitted – as evinced in *hadith; ijtihad* – analogical reasoning; and *ijma* – consensus of the community of legal scholars or religious authorities. The four schools of Sunni Islam (orthodox) are Hanafi, Hanbali, Maliki and Shafi'i (see below). Among Shi'ahs, the main school of jurisprudence is Jafari; however, in Yemen the Zaydi School is dominant (see below).

Shafi'i – one of the four Sunni (Orthodox) schools of Islamic jurisprudence. It first appeared in the central highlands of Yemen in 912-13 AD and is now dominant in the southern highlands, coastal areas and most of the former PDRY.

Sufi – a term for devotees of various mystical brands of Islam that developed from the 7th century AD. In Yemen they find expression among Shafi'is and condemnation among Zaydis. The first historical references to Sufism in Yemen were in the 12th century AD. Sufism is apolitical and inward focussing, with practices that strive for closeness to God, beauty of character and sincerity. It is believed that Yemeni Sufi mystics introduced both *qat* and coffee for human consumption.

Sultan – absolute ruler, or sovereign authority (from the Arabic root meaning might, strength, sovereign power or authority). A title used in south Arabia for specific local leaders, for example the Sultan of Lahj who was a powerful and wealthy ruler who owned one-sixth of all cultivated land in Lahj.[132]

'urf – customary or tribal law, from the root meaning 'to know or to be aware', referring to common knowledge embodied in age-old practices, precedence, agreements and the wisdom of judges and mediators. Transmitted to adult male tribe members through oral and written texts from generation to generation, at the most basic level *'urf* is designed to channel, minimise and resolve conflicts between individuals and groups.

wadi – watercourse or riverbed that is dry between Yemen's two annual monsoon seasons.

Zaydi – a branch of Shi'ah Islam established in Yemen by al-Hadi ila al-Haqq Yahya ibn Husayn in 896 AD, who was invited to Yemen as an arbitrator by local tribes. Al-Hadi's 14 years of leadership in Yemen inaugurated nearly 1,000 years of the Zaydi Imamate, which ruled various parts of Yemen until the 1962 Revolution (see Imam above). The Zaydi school of jurisprudence was established by Zayd ibn 'Ali, a grandson of Husayn, the fifth Imam.

Political actors

'Ali 'Abdullah Saleh – President of the YAR since 1978 and since unification in 1990 president of the ROY.

Bakil Confederation – a loose confederation of 12-14 tribes which, in contemporary times, have often aligned their interests with those of the Hashid Confederation (see below). The nominal Shaykh of the Bakil is Naji bin 'Abd al-'Aziz al-Shayif.

General People's Congress (GPC – *al-Mu'tamar al-Sha'abi al-'Amm*) – a political party created in 1982 in the YAR by President 'Ali 'Abdullah Saleh who has since served as its Secretary General. As the dominant partner in unification, the victor in the 1994 civil war and the strongest party in elected bodies, (parliament and the local councils) the GPC is a powerful political force in society, politics and the economy.

Hashid Confederation – comprises seven major tribes who were united and well organised during the 20th century. Since 1959 they have been led by Shaykh 'Abdullah bin Husayn al-Ahmar (referred to as their paramount *shaykh – shaykh al-mashayikh*), who also serves as the Speaker of the Parliament and the head of the Islah party.

Islah party – the abbreviated name of the Yemeni Reform Gathering (*al-tajammu' al-Yamani li-l-Islah*), founded in 1990. Islah has the second largest presence in parliament and its leader *Shaykh 'Abd Allah Ibn Husayn al-Ahmar* is head of the powerful Hashid Confederation as well as Speaker of the parliament since his overwhelming election in 1993.

Yemeni Socialist Party – (*Hizb al-Ishtiraqi al-Yemeni*) is the oldest political party on the Arabian Peninsula. Established in the 1950s as the National Liberation Front, it became the ruling party of the PDRY. It changed its name to the Yemeni Socialist Party in 1978.

Recommended resources

Recent films

The Hanging Gardens of Arabia 1990, 52 minutes. This film documents traditions in sustainable agriculture in Yemen and challenges facing these age-old practices. It focuses on environmental issues and how development cooperation can encourage sustainable traditions or destroy them. Produced by INCA/the Arid Lands Initiative. Available at: www.asgard.co.uk/mpa/equinox.htm.

Arab Women Speak Out 1997, 47 minutes. This documentary, training and advocacy project was designed to promote women's empowerment and engagement in social development throughout the Arab world. The film profiles several Yemeni women (and women from several other Arab countries) including Ibtisam 'Amer, a health professional and former Oxfam employee. Produced by Johns Hopkins University Center for Communication Programs. Available at: www.jhuccp.org/neareast/awso.

***Murshidat*, Midwives and Nurses: Muslim Women Transforming Health Care and Social Relations in Yemen** 1998, 40 minutes.
This documentary video highlights the female primary health care workers (*murshidat*) in the town of 'Abs who were trained as part of the ICD project. It follows the *murshidat* in their home visits and daily routines and shares their thoughts on the significance of their changing roles, achievements and aspirations. Produced by Dr Delores Walters, Colgate University. Available at: www.tang.outreach.psu.edu.

The Architecture of Mud 1999, 51 minutes.
A joint project of preservation from Pamela Jerome (Columbia University) and Caterina Borelli

(independent filmmaker), this documentary examines traditional methods of construction and preservation of mud brick masonry in the Wadi Hadhramaut. Produced by the American Institute for Yemeni Studies. Available at: www.der.org/docued.

An English Sheikh and a Yemeni Gentleman 2000, 75 minutes.
This documentary film introduces Bader Ben Hirsi, a British-born Yemeni living in London after his parents' exile from the Yemen, as he returns to rediscover his country, its people and traditions. Under the guiding hand of Englishman Tim Mackintosh-Smith, who has been living as a Yemeni in the ancient city of San'a' for the past 16 years, Ben Hirsi travels throughout his ancestral homeland. Produced by Bader Ben Hirsi. Available at: www.felixfilms.co.uk.

Books
The recent *Yemeni Voices: Women Tell Their Stories* provides a glimpse of the lives of **Yemeni women** and the development challenges they face. Edited by Marta Paluch and illustrated by the Yemeni artist Amnah Al-Nassiri (British Council, 2001) the publication was supported by the British government's Department for International Development (DFID).

For **general reading** and entertainment from a knowledgeable expert (the English Sheikh of the film above) see *Yemen: Travels in Dictionary Land* by Tim Mackintosh-Smith (John Murray, 1997). The same book is entitled *Yemen: The Unknown Arabia* for the US publication (Overlook Press, 2000).

Two books by Paul Dresch are excellent resources that provide insightful analysis of Yemeni **tribal traditions and history**: *Tribes, Government and History in Yemen* (Oxford University Press, 1989) and *A History of Modern Yemen* (Cambridge University Press, 2000).

For an entertaining and informative book on **qat** see *Eating the Flowers of Paradise: One Man's Journey Through Ethiopia and Yemen* by Kevin Rushby (IB Tauris, 1999).

Sheila Carapico's *Civil Society in Yemen: The Political Economy of Activism in Modern Arabia* (Cambridge University Press, 1998) provides excellent information on the **democratisation process** in Yemen and the modern history of civil society.

For an excellent book on Yemeni **architectural tradition** and the conservation of one of the country's most outstanding monuments see *The*

'Amiriya in Rada': The History and Restoration of a Sixteenth-Century Madrasa in the Yemen (Oxford University Press, 1997) by Selma al-Radi.

For breathtaking **coffee table books**, see the works of Pascal and Maria Marechaux, *Arabia Felix: Images of Yemen and its People* (Barron's, 1980), *Arabian Moons: Passages in Time Through Yemen* (Concept Media, 1987), *Yemen* (Dar al-Hikma al-Yamaniah, 1993) and *Impressions of Yemen* (Flammarion, 1997).

For an engaging readable book on **women's relationships** in Zabid, see Anne Meneley's *Tournaments of Value: Sociability and Hierarchy in a Yemen Town* (University of Toronto Press, 1996).

For a thorough reference work on Yemeni **history** see *Historical Dictionary of Yemen* by Robert D. Burrowes (Scarecrow Press, 1995).

For a detailed examination of **property, agriculture and traditional household relations** in a community outside San'a' see Martha Mundy's *Domestic Government: Kinship, Community and Polity in North Yemen* (IB Tauris, 1995).

For Yemeni **literature translated into English** there is Zayd Mutee' Dammaj's *The Hostage: A Novel* (Interlink Books, 1994); *They Die Strangers: A Novella and Stories from Yemen* by Mohammad Abdul-Wali (Centre for Middle Eastern Studies, University of Texas at Austin, 2001); and *The Adventures of Sayf Ben Dhi Yazan: An Arab Folk Epic*, translated and narrated by Lena Jayyusi (Bloomington and Indianapolis: Indian University Press, 1996).

Salma Samar Damluji's *A Yemen Reality: Architecture Sculptured in Mud and Stone* (Garnet Publishing, 1991) is an informative and detailed look at the **architectural traditions** of the Wadi Hadhramaut.

For a detailed and thoughtful look at **tribal poetry and culture** in Yemen see Steven Caton's *Peaks of Yemen I Summon: Poetry as Cultural Practice in a North Yemeni Tribe* (University of California Press, 1990).

The writing on the Hadhramaut of the intrepid Freya Stark still stands as a classic of **travel literature**. See *The Southern Gates of Arabia: A Journey in the Hadhramaut* (John Murray, 1936) and *A Winter in Arabia* (John Murray, 1945).

Although the books of Harold and Doreen Ingrams are not easy to find they are well worth the effort for their excellent insights into **South Yemen during the British era**, *Arabia and the Isles* (Frederick Praeger, 1966) and *The Yemen: Imams, Rulers and Revolutions* (John Murray, 1936) by

Harold Ingrams and *A Time in Arabia* (John Murray, 1970) by Doreen Ingrams.

For information on the history of **Yemeni communities in the United Kingdom**, see *From Ta'izz to Tyneside: An Arab Community in the North-east of England During the Early Twentieth Century* by Richard I Lawless (Univesity of Exeter Press, 1995); and *Arabs in Exile: Yemeni Migrants in Urban Britain* by Fred Halliday (IB Tauris, 1992).

Internet sites

The American Institute for Yemeni Studies (AIYS) has an excellent website providing information on the organisation and it links to the Yemen Webdate which has extensive information on Yemen including recent publications, films listings and much more. It also links to hundreds of other useful websites. At: www.aiys.org

Yemen Gateway includes up-to-date news on Yemen, analysis of politics and the economy as well as weather reports, excellent photos, tide tables for Aden, links to Prince Naseem Hamed websites, etc. At: www.al-bab.com/yemen

The Royal Botanical Gardens in Edinburgh has an excellent website that focuses on their work on the island of Soqotra which includes providing botanical and other services towards the production of the master development plan for the island. At: www.rbge.org.uk/ Arabia/Soqotra/home/page01.html

The Centre Français d'Archéologie et des Sciences Sociales de Sanaa (CEFAS) has an extensive website with an excellent array of articles and research information. At: www.univ-aix.fr/cfey

The British-Yemeni Society's website contains a rich collection of articles on Yemen, the organisation's activities and links to related websites. At: www.al-bab.com/bys

International NGOs working in Yemen

Adventist Development Relief Agency (ADRA) www.adra.org

American-Mideast Educational and Training Services (AMIDEAST) www.amideast.org/offices/yemen

CARE Australia www.careaustralia.com.au/yemen.htm

Friedrich Ebert Stiftung (FES) www.fes-yemen.com

ICD www.ciir.org

International Foundation for Election Systems (IFES) www.ifes.org/nearlist.htm

International Committee of the Red Cross (ICRC) www.icrc.org/icrceng.nsf/ CountryDetails?Readform&Country=Yemen

Marie Stopes International (MSI) www.mariestopes.org.uk/yemen.html

Médecins Sans Frontiéres (MSF) www.msf.org

National Democratic Institute (NDI) www.ndi.org/ndi/worldwide/mideast_noafrica/ Yemen

Oxfam UK www.oxfam.org.uk/atwork/where/asia/ mideast/yemen.htm

Radda Barnen (RB) www.rb.se/engindex.htm

Bibliography

Books and articles

Adra, Najwa (1985) 'The Concept of Tribe in Rural Yemen', in Hopkins, N and Ibrahim, S D (eds) *Arab Society: Social Science Perspectives*, Cairo, American University of Cairo, pp275–285.

— (1998) 'Dance and Glance: Visualizing Tribal Identity in Highland Yemen', *Visual Anthropology*, Vol. 11, pp55-102.

Al-Kamali, Mahyoob (2000) 'Economic Reforms of the 90s: Background, Objectives and Outcomes', *Yemen Times*, 29 May-4 June 2000.

Al-Maitami, Mohammed (1998a) 'Efforts of Economic Programme and Structural Adjustment,' a conference organised by the Centre for Contemporary Arab Studies, University of Georgetown, Washington, on October 1, 1998, at Yemen Gateway (www.al-bab.com/yemen).

— (1998b) *Reformative Process in the Market and State in Yemen*, a paper presented at the Middle East Studies Association Annual Meeting, Washington, DC, 6-10 December, at Yemen Gateway (www.al-bab.com/yemen).

Brunner, Ueli (1985) 'Irrigation and Land Use in the Ma'rib Region,' in *Economy, Society and Culture in Contemporary Yemen*, London, Croom Helm, pp51-63.

Buringa, Joke (1988) *Yemeni Women in Transition: How Development Cooperation Could Fit In*, Ministry of Foreign Affairs, Directorate General for International Cooperation, The Hague.

Burrowes, Robert D (1987) *The YAR: The Politics of Development 1962-1986*, Boulder, Westview Press.

— (1995a) 'The Yemeni Civil War of 1994: Impact on the Arab Gulf States,' in *The Yemeni War of 1994*, Abu Dhabi, Emirates Centre for Strategic Studies and Research, pp71-80.

— (1995b) *Historical Dictionary of Yemen*, Lanham/London, The Scarecrow Press, Inc.

Bury, G Wyman (1915/1998) *Arabia Infelix: Or the Turks in Yamen*, Reading, Garnet Publishing.

Carapico, Sheila (1993a) 'Elections and Mass Politics in Yemen,' *Middle East Report*, November-December, at: www.al-bab.com/yemen/pol/scarap.htm.

— (1996) *The Political Effects of Yemen's Structural Adjustment*, a paper presented at the Middle East Studies Association Annual Meeting, Providence, RI, 21-24 November.

— (1998) *Civil Society in Yemen: The Political Economy of Activism in Modern Arabia*. Cambridge, Cambridge University Press.

— (2000) 'Yemen and the Aden-Abyan Islamic Army', Press Information Notes, *Middle East Report*, at: www.merip.org/pin/pin35.html.

Clark, Janine A (1997) 'Women and Islamic Activism in Yemen' in *Yemen Update*, No. 39, American Institute for Yemeni Studies, pp13-15.

Dresch, Paul (1989) *Tribes, Government and History in Yemen*, Oxford, Clarendon Press.

— (1995) 'The Tribal Factor in the Yemeni Crisis' in *The Yemeni War of 1994*, Abu Dhabi, Emirates Centre for Strategic Studies and Research, pp33-55.

— (2000) *A History of Modern Yemen*, Cambridge, Cambridge University Press.

Gascoigne, Liz (1991) 'Finding Ways of Working With Women in Patriarchal Societies' in *Changing Perceptions: Writings on Gender and Development*, Oxford, Oxfam Print Unit, pp299-305.

Glander, Annelies (1998) *Inheritance in Islam: Women's Inheritance in Sana'a*, European University Studies, Series XXVII Asian and African Studies, Vol 69.

Gazzo, Yves (1999) 'The Specifics of the Yemeni Economy,' in *Le Yémen contemporain*, Centre Française d'Études Yéménites pp319-37.

Haddash, Saleh (1998) 'Human Rights System in Yemen', *Yemen Times*, 10-16 August, Issue 32, Vol VIII.

Halliday, Fred (1997) 'Arabia without Sultans Revisited', *Middle East Report*, July-September, Issue No. 204 at: www.merip.org/mer/mer204/halliday.html.

— (1999) *Oman and Yemen: An Historical Re-Encounter,* lecture to a joint meeting of the Anglo-Omani and British Yemeni Societies, 28 October.

Kemps, Annica and Staugard, Frantz (1992) *Quality of Maternal and Neo-natal Health Services in Yemen*, ROY, Radda Barnen.

Lackner, Helen (1985) *P.D.R. Yemen: Outpost of Socialist Development in Arabia*, London, Ithaca Press.

— (1995) 'Women and Development in the Republic of Yemen', in Gender and Development in the Arab World, London and New Jersey, ZED Books, Ltd.

Lowry, Robert and Henin, Nicolas (2000) 'Yemen: Armed to the Teeth', *Arabies Trends*, April, No. 30, pp50-52.

Manea, Elham M. (1998) 'Yemen, The Tribe and the State', at Yemen Gateway (www.al-bab.com/yemen).

Mernissi, Fatima (1993) *The Forgotten Queens of Islam*, Minneapolis, University of Minnesota Press.

Mundy, Martha (1995) *Domestic Government: Kinship, Community and Polity in North Yemen*, IB Tauris Publishers.

Nonneman, Gerd (1997) 'Key Issues in the Yemeni Economy', at: www.al-bab.com/yemen/econ.

Niebuhr, M (1792/1994) *Travels Through Arabia and Other Countries in the East, Vols I and II*, translated by Robert Heron, Reading, Garnet.

Saif, Ahmed 'Abdulkareem (1997) 'The Politics of Survival and the Structure of Control in the Unified Yemen 1990-97', at: www.al-bab.com/yemen/artic/art/htm.

RB Serjeant and Ronald Lewcock (eds) (1983) *San'a': An Arabian Islamic City*, London, The World of Islam Festival Trust.

Sadek, Noha (1993) 'In the Queen of Sheba's Footsteps: Women Patrons in Rasulid Yemen', in *Asian Art*, Vol VI, No. 2, Spring, University of Oxford Press, pp15-27.

Stookey, Robert W (1978) *Yemen: The Politics of the Yemen Arab Republic*, Boulder, Westview Press.

Walter, Delores M (1998) 'Invisible Survivors: Women and Diversity in the Transitional Economy of Yemen', in Lobban, Jr, Richard A (ed) *Middle Eastern Women and the Invisible Economy*, Gainesville, University of Florida Press, pp74-95.

Warburton, David A (1995) 'Women in Ancient Yemen', in *Yemen Update*, No. 36, American Institute for Yemeni Studies, pp23 and 33.

Wenner, Manfred (1967) *Modern Yemen 1918-1966*, Baltimore, Johns Hopkins Press.

Whitaker, Brian (1998) 'Favourable Ruling', *Middle East International*, 16 October, at Yemen Gateway (www.al-bab.com/yemen).

- (2000a) 'Commentary on the Yemeni-Saudi Border Agreement', at Yemen Gateway (www.al-bab.com/yemen).

— Whitaker (2000b) 'The International Dimension' at: www.al-bab.com/yemen/pol/bwint.htm.

Würth, Anna (1994) *The Legal Status of Women in Yemen*, Report to CID/WID Project, Tucson, AZ, University of Arizona.

— (1995) 'A Sana'a Court: The Family and the Ability to Negotiate', in *Islamic Law and Society*, 2, 3, Leiden, EJ Brill, pp320-40.

Other sources

Amnesty International (1997) 'Yemen: Ratification Without Implementation: The State of Human Rights in Yemen', at: www.amnesty.org.

— (1999) 'AI Report 1999: Yemen', at: www.amnesty.org.

Al-Bab.Com (1999) 'Security Incidents in Yemen 1990-94' and 'Security Incidents in Yemen 1998-1999', at www.al-bab.com/yemen/pol/pol.htm.

Children and Women in Yemen: A Situation Analysis 1998, Republic of Yemen, UNICEF, World Bank and Radda Barnen, Volumes I-IV, San'a'.

Federation of the Chambers of Commerce and Industry of Yemen (1998) *The View of the Private Sector on Administrative Functions*, a paper submitted to the National Conference for Administrative and Financial Reforms in Sana'a, Section 3.

Gender Policy on Agriculture and Food Security (1999) Rural Women's Development General Directorate, Ministry of Agriculture and Irrigation, Republic of Yemen, Royal Netherlands Embassy, June.

International Monetary Fund (1997) 'IMF Approves Combined ESAF/EFF Financing for the Republic of Yemen', Washington DC, October at: www.imf.org.

Middle East Watch (1992) *Yemen: Steps Toward Civil Society*, New York, New York.

National Report on the Implementation Level of the Convention on Elimination of all Forms of Discrimination Against Women, Women's National Committee, Republic of Yemen, December 1999.

National Women Committee (1999) *Report on the Status of Women in Yemen Five Years After Beijing 1995*, Republic of Yemen, San'a'.

Permanent Court of Arbitration 'Yemen and Eritrea: Hunaish Dispute Arbitration Ruling', 9 October 1998.

Republic of Yemen (2000) *The Interim Poverty Reduction Strategy Paper (IPRSP)*, San'a'.

United Nations Development Programme (2001) *Yemen Common Country Assessment*.

— (2000) *Human Development Report 2000*, New York.

— (2000) *Annual Report of the United Nations Resident Coordinator: Republic of Yemen*, San'a'.

— (March 1999) *Programme for Enhancement of Accountability, Transparency and Rule of Law*, San'a'.

— (1998) *Yemen: Human Development Report*, San'a'.

United Nations High Commissioner on Refugees (1999) 'The Middle: Yemen', at: www.unhcr.ch/world/mide/yemen.htm.

US Department of State (1996) 'Background Notes on Yemen' at: www.state.gov/www/background_notes/yemen_1096_bgn.html.

— (2000) *Yemen Report on Human Rights Practices for 1999*, February.

— (2001) *Yemen Report on Human Rights Practices for 2000*, February.

World Bank (1979) *PDRY: A Review of Economic and Social Development*.

— (1979) *YAR: Development of a Traditional Economy*

— (1993) *Republic of Yemen Agricultural Sector Study: Strategy for Sustainable Agricultural Production*, Vol II, Annexes and Statistical Data, Report No. 11126-YEM, September.

— (1997) *Yemen, Towards a Water Strategy: An agenda for Action*, Report No. 15718-YEM, Middle East and North Africa Region, Middle East Dept, Rural Development, Water and Environmental Sector, 13 August.

— (1999) *Agriculture Strategy Note, Report No. 17073-YEM*, May.

Yemen Observer (1999) 'Smuggling distorts Yemen's Economy', 1 October.

Yemen Times (1998) 'The Drying Up of Yemeni Tourism', 13-19 July, Issue 28, Vol VIII.

— (1999) 'Egypt and Yemen: Similarities and Differences', View Point, 7-15 February, Issue 7, Vol IX.

— (2000) 'Inhumane Crime in Private Jail', 24-30 April, Issue 17, Vol X.

— (2000) 'Budget Deficit Despite High Oil Prices',

ICD and CIIR

International Cooperation for Development (ICD) recruits experienced professional to share their skills in development projects in Latin America, the Caribbean, Southern Africa and Yemen. ICD is a programme of CIIR (Catholic Institute for International Relations), an independent charity which works in partnership with civil groups and governments to:

- secure just and equitable policies at national and international level
- build the capacity of community-based organisations that represent the interests of the poor and improve their quality of life.

CIIR has consultative status at the Economic and Social Council of the United Nations (ECOSOC). UK registered charity no. 294329

INTERNATIONAL
COOPERATION
FOR DEVEL●PMENT

CIIR/ICD Unit 3 Canonbury Yard
190a New North Road, London N1 7BJ, UK
Phone: +44 (0)20 7354 0883
Fax: +44 (0)20 7359 0017
www.ciir.org

Other publications from CIIR

Human Rights in Somaliland —
Awareness and action

The report of a workshop in Hargeisa, Somaliland,
17-19 October 1998
Amnesty International and International Cooperation for
Development

In 1998 in Hargeisa civil society activists met with journalists,
government representatives and lawyers to define the key human
rights issues in Somaliland. The workshop, organised jointly by
Amnesty International and International Cooperation for
Development, provided an unprecedented opportunity to
explore children's rights, human rights awareness, the rights of
women and minorities, justice and prison conditions. This report
documents the workshop. It will be of value to anyone with an
interest in human rights promotion, education and training, and
current developments in Somaliland.

52 pages £4.95 1999 ISBN 1852872225

Somaliland NGOs —
Challenges and opportunities
by Mohamed Sheik Abdillahi

The collapse of government and public services in Somalia as a
result of the country's civil war left a vacuum that has seen a
rapid growth in the number of local non-governmental
organisations. In the north-west regions, which seceded from
Somalia in 1991 to form the independent Republic of Somaliland,
local NGOs have played a key role in rehabilitation, governance,
security and reconciliation. In this paper, Mohamed Sheik
Abdillahi, an active member of the movement since its
beginnings, outlines the achievements of Somaliland's NGOs and
the many challenges facing them, including strained relations
with government and international bodies. He sets out
recommendations for local NGOs to realise their full potential in
the vast and urgent task of reconstructing their country virtually
from scratch.

8 pages £1.50 1997 ISBN 1852871970

Building Partnerships for Participatory Development
Report of a workshop held in Hargeisa, Somaliland

Sustained social and economic recovery in Somalia will depend on building a political consensus based on a common vision and shared values. In December 1995 Somali development workers organised a pioneering workshop in Hargeisa with representatives from local and international NGOs, community organisations and Somaliland's government to discuss the country's rehabilitation. This report describes the workshop, its objectives and methodology. It is an invaluable resource for development workers and NGOs interested in Somaliland and/or participatory development.

48 pages £9.95 1996 ISBN 1852871539

Building partnerships for Peace and Development
Report of a workshop held in Borama, Somaliland

This report details a workshop held in late 1996 to equip local NGOs with skills in conflict analysis and strategy building for peace and development. The workshop aimed to promote collaborative efforts between local NGOs as a means of fostering rehabilitation and development in Somaliland. It also aimed to contribute to the building of a viable local NGO movement. It provides a practical resource for local organisations planning similar initiatives. It traces the learning process of the workshop leaders, who took part in conflict resolution training in the UK, and describes how they shared their new skills with workshop participants.

58 pages £4.95 1997 ISBN 1852871962

HIV/AIDS in Southern Africa
The threat to development
by Helen Jackson, Russell Kerkhoven, Diane Lindsey,
Gladys Mutangadura, Fungayi Nhara
Comment series

Southern Africa is thought to have two-thirds of the world=s 30.6 million people living with HIV. More than 7 per cent of people aged 15-49 in the region are HIV positive, and 7.8 million children under the age of 15 in sub-Saharan Africa have been orphaned as a result of AIDS. The authors argue that HIV/AIDS needs to be tackled as a development issue, not just as a health concern. This Comment explores the scale of the epidemic, factors promoting it and the impact on development in the region. Includes an annotated bibliography.

64pp £2.50 1999 ISBN 1852872182

The authors work for the Southern Africa AIDS Information Dissemination Service (SAfAIDS), a regional NGO based in Zimbabwe.

We Will Not Dance On Our Grandparents Tombs

Indigenous uprisings in Ecuador
Kintto Lucas
Translated by Dinah Livingstone

In January 2000 Ecuador's indigenous people walked into the capital Quito where they demanded – and got – the resignation of the discredited president Jamil Mahuad. This was the latest in a history of levantamientos indígenas (Indian uprisings) going back to the early 1990s when resistance to celebrations of the 500th anniversary of Columbus' 'discovery' of the Americas had found voice in the slogan 'We will not dance on our grandparents' tombs'. This book brings together news articles covering the levantamientos in 1999 and 2000 with interviews with indigenous leaders to provide a unique insight into one of the strongest and most politically sophisticated civil movements in Latin America.

120 pages £8.95 2000 ISBN 1852872365
Kintto Lucas is a Uruguayan journalist living and working in Ecuador.

A catalogue of CIIR publications is available from the address below.

For more information or to place an order visit www.ciir.org
Or contact:

Publications Section,
CIIR, Unit 3 Canonbury Yard
190a New North Road,
London N1 7BJ, UK
Phone +44 (0)20 7354 0883
Fax +44 (0)20 7359 0017
sales@ciir.org